MW00889461

PURSUE
ONENESS

Seven Key
Strategies to the
Relationship of
Your Dreams

DR. MICHAEL & AMY SMALLEY
ROGER GIBSON

Smalley Institute
26205 Oak Ridge Drive, Suite 119
The Woodlands, TX 77380

www.smalleyinstitute.com

Ordering Information:

Quantity sales. Special discounts are available on quantity purchases by corporations, associations, and others. For details, contact the publisher at the address above.

Orders by U.S. trade bookstores and wholesalers. Please contact us at (800) 975-8748.

Previous works

Books:

Don't Date Naked
More than a Match
DNA of Relationships
Men's Relational Toolbox
Communicating with your Teen
The Surprising Way to a Stronger Marriage

Video Series:

Secrets to Lasting Love
Five Keys to Better Kids
DNA of Relationships
The Surprising Way
Pursue Online Course

WANT FREE RELATIONSHIP ADVICE?

WEEKLY PODCASTS

FREE ONLINE COURSES

EMAIL ONLY DISCOUNTS AND SPECIALS

PRIZES, CONTESTS & MORE

SIGN UP TODAY AT WWW.SMALLEYINSTITUTE.COM

Like Us!

Follow Us!

SCAN WITH

BARCODE SCANNER

TO LIKE

facebook.com/MichaelandAmy

SCAN WITH

BARCODE SCANNER

TO FOLLOW

twitter.com/Michael_Smalley

Table of Contents

Dedication

There are many, incredible people who help get a book published! We are merely the authors, who had a dream, to publish a book that couples might read so that marriages might be helped.

First, we want to thank our amazing team of marriage coaches. The Smalley Institute brand is only as strong as you help us make it. There are many testimonies of couples you have worked with that saw their marriages reignited because you helped them apply our concepts.

To Wendy Baldwin, VP of Operations, you are the glue that holds our company together. You are truly one in a million. Your dedication to our business is unsurpassed. Thank you to Eddie Baldwin for being Wendy's calm in the storm when we drive her crazy.

Thanks to our intensive coordinator Isabel Peralez. You are the first impression our couples have, and we are so proud of the work you do. To Jeanine Holloway, for taking so many service calls and for the passion in how you serve our ministry.

And last but not least, our kids Cole, Reagan, and David… through the adventures of homeschooling, following us around the globe, and manning our book tables. We love you so very much.

Why Pursue?

My (Michael) father spent nearly 50 years inspiring couples to build a better relationship. His first marriage seminar was called "Love is a Decision". It revolutionized marriage ministry and marriage education.

Pursue Oneness comes from the heritage and legacy of Dr. Gary Smalley, but it takes the next step in the evolution of what it means to build the marriage of your dreams. Everything in this book is designed and proven through marriage ministry in the local church. All three of us work in the church and through the church to inspire couples and help them build community so they never have to face the devastating effects of divorce.

If you are going to build the kind of marriage that stands the test of time, culture, children, in-laws, finances, poor communication and misunderstanding then you must pursue Christ as you pursue oneness. Perhaps the greatest verses on love are found in 1 Corinthians 13. We know you have heard or read these verses before, but our hope is you will see the words in a fresh way as they lead you down the path of pursuing oneness. Pay special attention to the verses where we add emphasis:

> **Love Is the Greatest**
> If I could speak all the languages of earth and of angels, **but didn't love others**, I would only be a noisy gong or

a clanging cymbal. If I had the gift of prophecy, and if I understood all of God's secret plans and possessed all knowledge, and if I had such faith that I could move mountains, **but didn't love others**, I would be nothing. If I gave everything I have to the poor and even sacrificed my body, I could boast about it; **but if I didn't love others**, I would have gained nothing.

Love is patient and kind. Love is not jealous or boastful or proud or rude. It does not demand its own way. It is not irritable, and it keeps no record of being wronged. It does not rejoice about injustice but rejoices whenever the truth wins out. Love never gives up, never loses faith, is always hopeful, and endures through every circumstance.

Prophecy and speaking in unknown languages and special knowledge will become useless. **But love will last forever!** Now our knowledge is partial and incomplete, and even the gift of prophecy reveals only part of the whole picture! But when the time of perfection comes, these partial things will become useless.

When I was a child, I spoke and thought and reasoned as a child. But when I grew up, I put away childish things. Now we see things imperfectly, like puzzling reflections in a mirror, but then we will see everything with perfect clarity. All that I know now is partial and incomplete, but then I will know everything completely, just as God now knows me completely.

Three things will last forever—faith, hope, and love— **and the greatest of these is love**.

Pursue Oneness … Pursue in Greek is: διώκω,ν \{dee-o'-ko}

> *to make to run or flee, put to flight, drive away 2) to run swiftly in order to catch a person or thing, to run after 2a) to press on: figuratively of one who in a race runs swiftly to reach the goal 2b) to pursue (in a hostile manner) 3) in any way whatever to harass, trouble, molest one 3a) to persecute 3b) to be mistreated, suffer persecution on account of something 4) without the idea of hostility, to run after, follow after: someone 5) metaph., to pursue 5a) to seek after eagerly, earnestly endeavor to acquire*

Why Pursue Oneness? Because nothing is more important in life than loving God and loving others. This book is about you pressing in, never giving up and running after each other and the blessing of loving one another like Jesus loves you!

In 1999, the Smalley family and a team of experts on our staff began to evaluate how couples in crisis were being helped. At our live events, we continually had couples approach us and say, "We've read books that were great, this seminar was great, but we need more help…what else do you have?"

Truly struggling couples found it difficult to apply the principles in our books and live events to their specific relationship. We knew traditional marital counseling wasn't the way to go, because it tends to have a low success rate in helping couples stay together. My (Michael's) brother, Dr. Greg Smalley, championed a team of psychology professionals down a path of marriage education done in an intensive format. Thus, the first marriage intensive movement was born in Branson, Missouri.

After years of continually honing the program and researching its effectiveness, we landed on a two to three day, private format, that would give a couple 14-21 hours of marriage education in a much shorter time period than traditional marriage counseling. We found that by doing this, couples experienced much greater success.

While we tailor every private intensive to the individual couple, we know that not every couple can attend one. And, we wanted as many couples as possible to have access to the content that we share during a two-day intensive. **You are holding that in your hands right now**.

What we know is what we do works. Over 85% of the couples that go through the Smalley Marriage Intensive Program stay together and significantly increase in marital satisfaction. **Over 99% of the people who experience one of our intensives would recommend it to another couple or family member needing help!**

The Study Guide

One of the best ways you could experience the content and skills taught in this book is through a small group, class or mentoring relationship. For those of you who might not know what a small group is, in essence, it's a gathering of at least three couples (and up to five couples max) who commit to meeting once a week at each other's homes. You get to journey through this book with other couples and use the discussion guide as a means to go deeper into the skills and concepts taught in the book.

Often the best place to get connected to a small group or class is at your local church. If you don't belong to a church, you can also connect with couples who are friends of yours and who would want to meet weekly to discuss both the book and the lessons being taught. Growing a great marriage happens in a community. We encourage every couple to join a small group to strengthen their relationship with God and one another.

At the end of a chapter, you will notice a study guide section. The study guide can be done in a group study, like we discussed above, or done as a couple. There will be discussion questions to help you process what you just read and any new concepts or breakthroughs discovered.

The Activity Section
The activities are going to be some of the most important things you do during this study. They are meant to be done on

separate days. The activities allow you to put into action what you are learning through the book and discussion time with your group or mentor. We also encourage you to journal, a lot, through this study. Do not ignore journaling your thoughts and experiences before or after an activity.

Journal Activity

Each week, we ask what you are learning. This is important because if you are not asking yourself what you are discovering throughout the book and study, then you are missing out on important revelations for your relationship. Take the time to journal. You will not regret it.

How To Experience The Best Out Of This Book

There are possibly two types of people reading this book. The first type is someone who is in crisis with his or her partner and is looking for help, trying to turn a hurting relationship around. The second type of person is someone who is in a good relationship and wants to keep the good times rolling. This book is good for both types! But you will want to keep a few critical things in mind depending on which type you are.

If you are needing help or in crisis:

1. Do all the activities each week. These are not optional activities and they are a critical part of keeping you moving forward in your marriage.
2. Keep positive and focus on what you want to add to your marriage, not the negative.

3. Find people to talk to…. a mentor couple (two people older and wiser than you) or invite another couple (but one who is healthy and vibrant) to go through this study together. Having another couple invested in your success is a big part of why this study is going to make a major, positive impact in your marriage. You can also do this study with a trained professional counselor as well.

If you are doing well as a couple:

1. This study can certainly be done with just the two of you. But our biggest dream is to encourage you to find a small group to go through this study. You can buy the curriculum and even get online training on how to become a facilitator or mentor (check it out here www.smalleyinstitute.com/p/marriage-mentor-training)! Make sure and allow a consistent time each week for meeting and going through the activities and discussions with each other.

2. Do all the activities, even if you don't feel like they apply to your situation. You can always learn from anything you do in this study, but it also helps you be a better mentor couple (one day) if you've gone through it yourself.

3. If something difficult comes up during the course of this study, don't panic. Just be thankful and bring in a mentor or close friend to help work through any issues.

For Marriage Mentors

If you've been asked to walk through this book with another couple or friend, then congratulations! Your marriage gets to benefit from serving and guiding another couple through this book and study!

In order to be the best mentor/friend you can be, please know the best thing you can do for their relationship is be authentic. There's no reason to hide or ignore your own issues, because no one is perfect, and most of the time, it is your past failures that will be the biggest teacher for other couples.

Here are a few more good tips to being a great mentor/friend:

1. Be Committed

There might be a time during this book where your commitment and desire for the couple's success is all that is keeping them together! Make sure and frequently share your belief and desire for the success of their marriage and their future.

2. Be An Example

Make sure your own marriage is on the right track. If you are not doing well in your own marriage, you will not be able to help the couple at all. We cannot take people farther than we have gone ourselves. You need to be able to show them what a good marriage looks like, not a perfect marriage, but at least a happy one!

3. Be Honest (Especially When It Is Hard)

If there is something that needs to be confronted in the couple (or individual), then please do not ignore it or shy away from it. You've already been given permission to speak into the couple's life because they asked you to do this book with them!

4. Be An Educator

Remember, most couples get into trouble because they do not know how to have a healthy, satisfying marriage. Teaching is a critical part of this book because the couple is getting the chance to learn what it takes to build a happy marriage.

You Don't Have To Be A Therapist

One of the reasons couples might hesitate on becoming a marriage mentor for another couple is they think being a professional therapist is needed to help other couples.

This is not true!

Actually, the best way to help a couple get unstuck and back on track in their relationship is to simply be there for them and be an accountability partner for them.

Your biggest job in helping another couple is agreeing to meet with them weekly for no more than two hours to help keep them accountable to what they are discovering in this book.

Your role each week is to:

- Encourage positive behavior and validate feelings (you might need to skip ahead and read this skill)... Your goal should be to see the good and nurture it.
- Ask the couple if they did the activities in each chapter.
  - If they did, then focus on the positives and help clear up any confusion from the chapter they might have.
  - If they didn't, then ask what got in the way of them completing the activities and encourage them to work through them with you there to coach if they get stuck.
- Join in the discussion from the chapter and share what you learned after reading it. In turn, allow them to share what they learned. You teach by sharing with you have learned.

Introduction

GOALS FOR THIS CHAPTER

Understanding:
- The importance of this book for your relationship
- The power of marriage education
- The journey you will experience through this book

"Great marriages don't just happen any more than accomplished musicians become that way by accident."
              Jimmy Evans, in the *Lifelong Love Affair*

Laura Smith had been suspicious of her husband for months. The signs weren't obvious, but there were signs nonetheless. Late nights at the office, longer than expected business trips, an absurd need for privacy with his phone, because as he would tell her, "I've got sensitive client issues you can't see." He guarded that phone like Fort Knox, never letting it out of his sight and making sure it was always password protected with four digits only he knew.

Laura and Jeff came to the Smalley Marriage Intensive because their relationship was suffering. They were not connecting, always fighting, and then this business about a possible affair hung over their marriage like a dark thundercloud. Jeff denied any possibility of an affair. Laura was having difficulty believing him.

The Smiths were unhappy to say the least.

We created the Smalley Marriage Intensive for the Smiths and for any couple struggling to get along. Let us explain why.

You may not be aware of how important this book is for your relationship. Communities like Modesto, CA, have experienced a decline of nearly 50% in their divorce rate because they started learning the key skills necessary to love well. Those skills are contained throughout this book! A great relationship is no longer a mystery, and you are about to learn the most fundamental elements to a thriving relationship.

What's the secret? Marriage education. We realize this phrase is unexciting, maybe a tad bland. You were hoping for something sexier, more mysterious, more . . . more anything! Who wants *education* to be the secret to a successful relationship? People want passion, romance, great sex, fun times, big houses, fancy cars, or obedient children to be the big secret! But these things don't matter when it comes to your overall happiness in your relationship. What matters is how much knowledge and skill you possess on HOW to love well. Love is a skill. It is not an emotion. It is not chemistry. It is a daily choice you make to care, be patient, forgiving, kind, gracious, and serving to the most important people in your life. Especially when they don't deserve love.

The Heritage Foundation did a massive study on the effectiveness of marriage education when former President George W. Bush signed the Healthy Marriage Initiative into action. "One analysis, integrating 85 studies, involving nearly 4,000 couples who were enrolled in more than 20 different marriage enrichment programs, found that the average couple, after participating in a program, was better off than more than two-thirds of couples that did not participate." [1] That's a mouthful of numbers and data; so let me (Michael) break it down for you. For those of you, like me, who don't fully understand fractions, two-thirds means over 66% of couples are worse off in their relationship than couples who participate in marriage education, or learning how to better love each other.

Great relationships are no accident. They take work. You need the knowledge and skill to successfully navigate the ups and downs of your relationship's journey through life. If you want to succeed, if you want to be happy together, then keep moving forward and apply all you learn in this book to your relationship, because this book offers the key elements to success from our Smalley Marriage Intensive Program for couples.

Since 2001, couples from across the globe have participated in the Smalley Marriage Intensive. The Smalley Institute continues to grow in identifying and learning what it takes to

---

[1] "Marriage and welfare reform: the overwhelming evidence that marriage education works." Patrick F. Fagan, Robert W. Patterson, & Robert E. Rector

help couples experience the relationship of their dreams, even if they've experienced:

- affairs
- broken promises
- in-laws
- financial breakdowns
- bitterness
- unmet expectations
- and other hurts

We survey and research the couples that attend the Smalley Marriage Intensive Program because it is important for us to know whether Pursue actually helps couples in their relationship.

The benefits of our Smalley Marriage Intensive are now available in this book. You get to learn what it takes to be successful before things get out-of-control. It's like a vaccination against break-up for your relationship!

All it takes is a willingness to change.

A man walked into the office recently with a great question. "Can people really change? I am old and set in my ways," (his words not ours). "I don't think I can change at this point in my life." He was feeling unloved AND unlovable. In a way, it seemed like he was saying, "People don't change… I am who I am, and there's nothing she can do but put up with me or go find someone else."

The problem with believing we don't or can't change is that we'd all be crawling around like babies or overreacting like teenagers if we couldn't change. We are complex human beings who have feelings and intellect, making change almost impossible to avoid. We change and our world changes. In the early nineties, we could connect to a mere 50 websites. But can you imagine life without the Internet now[2]? Life does *change* and we adapt. *How* we change is up to us. So if we *can* change what causes us to change?

We believe there are three common ways people change; through awareness, pain, and love.

Awareness seems the simplest and easiest way to affect change. Much of our work in the Smalley Marriage Intensive is awareness and education based. We take what we have learned over the years and apply it to their situation. Couples don't know how to communicate or resolve conflict, so we teach them – we make them aware.

Henry Cloud, a noteworthy author on relationships says this; "We change our behavior when the pain of staying the same becomes greater than the pain of changing. Consequences give us the pain that motivates us to change."[3]

---

[2] William Jefferson Clinton, "The Struggle for the Soul of the Twenty-First Century," NPQ: New Perspective Quarterly 19 (Spring 2002):30

[3] Henry Cloud, "goodreads.com/quotes/163723" May 6, 2014

Does pain cause you to change? Sometimes, right? Haven't you ever thought, "I'll never do that again. That was too painful." Many times pain is the best motivation to stop painful experiences from happening again.

The funny thing about how pain relates to love and relationships is this: most of us are hardwired to need love so much, we will keep trying, despite any pain we may have experienced. So even when someone hurts us, we either seek a way to feel loved or learn to numb out that need altogether, all for the sake of the relationship. We often see couples that have learned to cover up their needs with addictions and other destructive patterns of behavior, instead of working through the pain to find resolution.

So sometimes pain doesn't always cause change then? That's right! Sometimes the greatest motivation for change is love.

One of the best depictions of love changing the direction of someone's life is in *Les Miserables.*

"In Les Miserables, the convict Jean Valjean spent a night at the Bishop's house from which, in his fear and desperation, he stole some silver place settings and fled. Apprehended by police, Jean Valjean was returned to the Bishop's house to answer for his new crime.

However, Bishop Bienvenue sensed that this crime was paltry next to the real crime – the 19 years stolen from Jean Valjean's life – and a few silver settings did not even begin to atone for that. So, to the dismay of police and the astonishment of Jean Valjean, the Bishop declared the silver to be a gift freely given, and then threw in two silver candlesticks that the Bishop claimed Jean Valjean had left behind in error.

It was an act of altruism and kindness that in the ensuing years set in motion Jean Valjean's transformation into a man of heroic virtue who in turn would transform others."[4]

When love walks into the shadows of our lives, we feel we can overcome. Love motivates hope for a brighter day. When someone truly believes you are lovable, you want to rise to that love. Love gives us energy to change. Valjean's life was changed by one encounter with unmerited grace and love. Sometimes that's all it takes and other times it takes many encounters for love to make the difference. Our hope is that Pursue Oneness couples feel cared for (loved) first, and from there they have the energy to both understand the pain they cause and choose to change.

So What Now?

"What you need to know about the past is that no matter what has happened, it has all worked together to bring you to this very moment. And this is the moment you can choose to make everything new." Author Unknown

---

[4]Macrae, Gordon. http://thesestonewalls.com/gordon-macrae/les-miserables-the-bishop-and-the-redemption-of-jean-valjean/. January 23, 2013.

Your time in this book is going to be as productive as you make it. The question is…why are you reading this book? Is it to make a good relationship even better? Are you reading this book to move forward and repair your relationship from hurt? Or are you here to check off a box in order to say to yourself and others, "I did everything I could, not even that book helped us."

We hope you are here to make things better and to become a better partner. It is about building skills. No one is born ready to thrive in relationships. It takes knowledge and skills! I (Roger) like watching the Food Network. Every time I get into one of those chef shows, I feel inspired to cook and my expectation is that I will turn out the kind of cuisine the professional chef did on the show...never quite works out that way! I might want to be a great chef, but my skills aren't quite ready yet. I have not had enough practice with the new things I'm learning watching the Food Network.

The same is true for you. If you think your relationship is going to be perfect after finishing this book, think again. It takes some time to hone the skills you are discovering in this book. We are helping you get on the right track, but you need to be committed to the long term. Committed to applying the skills and practicing them day in and day out.

If you want to turn your relationship around, and make it happier than ever before, then you must be here to change and do things differently. If you are not here to change and fix this relationship, then you must be honest now. If you are all in, then say it. If you are not, then please say that as well.

Take a moment to sign on the dotted line. Are you in or out in making your relationship the best possible?

Please sign on the signature page to the right, below the number of your choice.

1. I'm all in and want to learn how to love better.

x..

Why?

_____

_____

2. I'm on the fence but I want to be open to change.

x..

Why?

_____

_____

3. I'm out and don't want to repair this relationship.

x..

Why?

_____

_____

You might be wondering why we'd ask you to sign such a statement. We've learned something in almost two decades of helping couples. If you want to learn and get better, you will. But if you are not taking the process seriously or have already checked out of the relationship…no program, no book, no counselor can help you.

If you keep your eyes on Jesus, the struggles or missteps in your relationship are going to be put in perspective. Jesus will give you the strength to keep going. In fact, that's a promise!

> 'Therefore, since we are surrounded by such a huge crowd of witnesses to the life of faith, let us strip off every weight that slows us down, especially the sin that so easily trips us up. And let us run with endurance the race God has set before us. We do this by keeping our eyes on Jesus, the champion who initiates and perfects our faith. Because of the joy awaiting him, he endured the cross, disregarding its shame. Now he is seated in the place of honor beside God's throne. '
> Hebrews 12:1-2

So be honest. Even if honesty feels scary, be honest. The reality is that your partner already knows you've checked out. You can't hide the true intentions of your heart. You are not fooling anyone. Be honest and gracious enough to allow your partner to know where you are and if you hope that will change.

Please understand, we believe there is no relationship beyond repair, given the right changes. "God can do anything, you know—far more than you could ever imagine or guess or request in your wildest dreams! He does it not by pushing us around but by working within us, his Spirit deeply and gently within us." Ephesians 3:20 MSG.

It might feel like an impossibility now, but that can change as you begin to read. The problem of divorce is that it doesn't really solve anything. It shadows some problems and creates more problems. If divorce were a good solution to a bad relationship, then second marriages would be more successful, right? But that's not the case... Second marriages fail more than first marriages. Depending on who produces the study, the rate is always above 50% but goes up to 60-67%. The point is this, divorce doesn't teach us how to choose a better mate. It teaches us how to divorce, and once that bridge has been crossed, it makes it easier and easier to do it again.

Your relationship can change. The secret is YOU learning what it takes to make a great relationship. If you are waiting for your partner to change, it might be a while. But when you change, the relationship changes.

Now it's time to move forward. If you decided to stick with the process of this book, then let's decide what your goals are for reading Pursue.

What do you want to accomplish through this book? Please list your goals below in the space provided. Keep this discussion about yourself and minimize any need to blame, criticize or shame your partner. You wouldn't want a goal that read something like, "My goal is for my husband to get a clue and stop working so much!" Think of goals more like, "I hope to better communicate after this book," or "My goal is to resolve a specific conflict using the tools in this book."

My goals

_____

_____

_____

_____

_____

When you have a clear picture of what you want from this book, you will get it. Knowing where you are headed and what you are hoping to gain makes all the difference in the world to the success of reading Pursue.

As you learn the skills in this book, apply them to the goals you listed here. Come back to this page as much as you need in order to stay focused on what you want to accomplish in your relationship.

Thank you for letting us walk alongside you. Our goal is to help you turn the struggles in your relationship into win/win solutions. As you begin the book, it's important to keep the following in mind:

- This book will be life changing.
- Be transparent and honest throughout the chapters.
- Stay open to the process and utilize this opportunity to focus solely on your relationship.
- Remember, the definition of insanity is doing the same thing over and over again and hoping for a different outcome. **Look for things you can change from this book and change them.**

It's time to get started.

> For I am about to do something new.
> See, I have already begun! Do you not see it?
> I will make a pathway through the wilderness.
> I will create rivers in the dry wasteland.
> Isaiah 43:19

Pursue God Together

Matthew 19:4-8

> "'Haven't you read the Scriptures?" Jesus replied.
> "They record that from the beginning 'God made them
> male and female.'" And he said, "'This explains why a
> man leaves his father and mother and is joined to his
> wife, and the two are united into one.' Since they are
> no longer two but one, let no one split apart what God
> has joined together." "Then why did Moses say in the
> law that a man could give his wife a written notice of
> divorce and send her away?" they asked. Jesus replied,
> "Moses permitted divorce only as a concession to your
> hard hearts, but it was not what God had originally
> intended.'

Why is it important for a man and woman to leave their father
and mother?

Jesus said that Moses only permitted divorce because of the people's hard hearts. What does a hard heart look and feel like? Secondly, what was God's original plan for marriage (see Genesis 1:26-27)?

_____

_____

_____

_____

How is God speaking to you through Matthew 19:4-8?

_____

_____

_____

_____

What are you going to do in response to Matthew 19:4-8?

_____

_____

_____

_____

1 Corinthians 13:11 "When I was a child, I spoke and thought and reasoned as a child. But when I grew up, I put away childish things."

This verse is referring to the opposite of love. Childish behavior is being impatient, unkind, jealous, arrogant, rude, irritable, gives up and keeps record of our partner's mistakes. But an adult pursues oneness, being intentional to choose actions that reflects Jesus. Making a decision to be kind when our partner may belittle us in front of the kids.

After reading 1 Corinthians 13:11, describe how a child loves vs. how an adult loves?

How a Child Love   How an Adult Loves

For example:

Arrogant   Humble

_____   _____

_____   _____

_____   _____

_____   _____

Prayer:

> Father, thank you for having a perfect plan for marriage and giving us the ultimate example of commitment. You are a God of unfailing faithfulness who loves unconditionally.
>
> Please help us to have an understanding of your plan for marriage, both when times are good and when they are challenging. Give us wisdom through the years as we walk through what seem to be insurmountable challenges so that we can ultimately experience the fullness of all that you intended marriage to be.

How Healthy Is Your Relationship?

GOALS FOR THIS CHAPTER

You will:
- Assess the overall health of your relationship
- Learn how to move forward

"It is not a lack of love, but a lack of friendship that makes unhappy marriages."
> Friedrich Nietzsche

"…since they are no longer two but one, let no one split apart what God has joined together." Mark 10:8-9

What would you think if we told you there is an eight question test that can predict divorce 93% accurately? Our guess is you would think something like, "Are you serious! Why would I want to find out if my marriage is headed for divorce? Clearly it is not healthy, or we wouldn't be here in the first place! Why would we take this test?"

It is understandable for you to be nervous, or even terrified at finding out if your relationship is healthy. But there's way more to the test than just that. It not only assesses the health of your relationship, it predicts divorce 93% accurately[5].

By now you are probably thinking, "Ok, now I'm closing this book for sure…no way do I want to find out if my marriage is going to end in divorce!"
Don't close the book quite yet.

If you are nervous, you may be operating with false negative beliefs about the assessment. Yes, the assessment does predict divorce accurately, but no, **it does not mean you are destined for divorce**.

Consider this assessment as a huge gift for your relationship. "A gift," you ask? Yes, a gift. You get to discover how healthy your relationship is and do something with what you discover! If you score in the green, then all systems go, your relationship is healthy and functioning as it should. If you score in the yellow, be careful, there are certain patterns emerging in how you handle conflict that may lead you in to trouble. **If you score in the red, then let it stand as a major warning that how you handle conflict is destructive and, if not changed, will lead to divorce!**

Notice the words in bold right above this sentence. If not changed…The gift of this assessment is that you get to discover where your relationship is, and what you can do to address any issues. If you score in the yellow or red, you now

---

[5] Research conducted by Dr. Scott Stanley and Dr. Howard Markman for the Smalley Institute

have a chance to fix it with the principles, tools, and skills in this book!

The assessment isn't a death sentence, but a chance to resurrect your relationship by changing key patterns in how you handle conflict.

The foundation to any healthy relationship is taking responsibility for your part. If you focus on your partner or significant other, things get worse. Let us say that again. If you focus on your partner or significant other (instead of yourself), things get worse. But, if you focus on what you can do to be the best you possible, things are set up to get better. In the end, you can't lose in life or relationships when you do the right thing.

It's time to gauge your relationship. Finding out where you stand is a good thing. No, wait . . . it's a great thing! How can you get better if you don't know what's going on? No matter what your score is, there's action you can take to keep it strong or make it even better!

THE EIGHT-QUESTION RELATIONSHIP ASSESSMENT

Years ago, we helped Dr. Howard Markman and Dr. Scott Stanley from the University of Denver validate an eight question test they developed by using it with over 100,000 couples! They found, based on the eight questions, that they could predict divorce nearly 93% accurately! That's right, with just eight questions, they were able to accurately predict whether a relationship was headed toward a break-up.

Dr. Markman and Dr. Stanley were able to predict divorce accurately because they know exactly what causes divorce. We will get into these four risk factors of divorce later in the book, but for now, we want you to realize there are really only four types of responses that lead to divorce.

The four factors of divorce are each represented by two statements in the assessment you are about to take. Don't be nervous, but remember you can change the direction of your relationship at any time. You might score poorly today, that doesn't mean you are going to score poorly 30 days from now.

THE EIGHT-QUESTION RELATIONSHIP ASSESSMENT

Take the following simple test to see to what extent these hazards have invaded your relationship. Read each of the statements listed below, and write down the number that best describes how often you feel you and your partner experience what the statements describe.

Use a three-point scale:

   1 = almost never; 2 = once in a while; 3 = frequently

   The assessment begins on the next page.

1 = almost never; 2 = once in a while; 3 = frequently

#	Factor
1	When we argue, one of us withdraws, not wanting to talk about it anymore, or leaves the scene.
1	Little arguments escalate into ugly fights, with accusations, criticisms, name calling, or bringing up past hurts.
2	My partner criticizes or belittles my opinions, feelings, or desires.
2	My partner seems to view my words or actions more negatively than I mean them to be.
1	When we have a problem to solve, it is as if we are on opposite teams.
1	I hold back from telling my partner what I really think and feel.
1	I think seriously about what it would be like to date or marry someone else.
1	I feel lonely in this relationship.
10	**Total Score** (add up the sum of the "Numbers" column)

What Does This Mean?

These statements, aimed at identifying the communication and conflict-management patterns that predict trouble in a relationship, are based on fifteen years of research from Drs. Markman and Stanley. The average score for couples was 11.

The Interpretations

Green Light: Score of 8–12

If you scored in the 8–12 range, your relationship is probably in good or even great shape at this time. We emphasize, "at this time," because relationships never stand still. In the next twelve months, you'll have either a stronger, happier relationship or one sliding in the other direction. If you scored in this range, think of it as a green light for now and keep moving forward to make your relationship all it can be.

Yellow Light: Score of 13–17

If you scored in the 13–17 range, think of it as a yellow caution light. While you may feel happy in your relationship, your score reveals warning signs, pointing to patterns you don't want to get worse. You ought to take action to protect and improve what you have. Spending time to strengthen your relationship now could be the best thing you could do for your future together.

Red Light: Score of 18–24

If you scored in the 18–24 range, think of it as a red light. Stop and look at where the two of you are headed. Your score indicates the presence of patterns that could put your relationship at significant risk. You may be heading for trouble —or perhaps you're already there. But there is good news! You can stop now and learn ways to improve your relationship. If your dream is turning into a nightmare, don't just pull the sheets over your head. Wake up and take action!

At this point, you may be thinking there is no way you can do this on your own. It's okay if you feel that way. You may want to contact us to see about the Smalley Marriage Intensive Program. We can be reached at 800-975-8748.

But if you're ready, continue moving forward.

Pursue God Together

Read the following scriptures:

> 'I pray that God, the source of hope, will fill you
> completely with joy and peace because you trust in him.
> Then you will overflow with confident hope through
> the power of the Holy Spirit.'
> Romans 15:13

> Don't be afraid, for I am with you.
> Don't be discouraged, for I am your God.
> I will strengthen you and help you.
> I will hold you up with my victorious right hand.
> Isaiah 41:10

If you scored in the yellow or red category, how do these
scriptures apply to your relationship?

_____

_____

_____

_____

We want the two of you to spend the next few minutes meditating on Psalms 121. Read through it one time, then ask the Lord to reveal any truth he wants you to understand. Now read it once more, but more slowly and deliberately. Paying close attention to what the Lord might be wanting to speak to you both.

Let the final, and third reading, be a prayer for your relationship.

> 'I look up to the mountains— does my help come from there? My help comes from the Lord , who made heaven and earth! He will not let you stumble; the one who watches over you will not slumber. Indeed, he who watches over Israel never slumbers or sleeps. The Lord himself watches over you! The Lord stands beside you as your protective shade. The sun will not harm you by day, nor the moon at night. The Lord keeps you from all harm and watches over your life. The Lord keeps watch over you as you come and go, both now and forever.'
>
> Psalms 121:1-8

How does God want you both to respond to each other after spending some time focused on Psalms 121?

_____

_____

Your Personality

GOALS FOR THIS CHAPTER

You will discover:
- Who you are
- How to love each other's unique personality styles
- Your own personality profile and what it means

"Always dream and shoot higher than you know you can do. Do not bother just to be better than your contemporaries or predecessors. Try to be better than yourself."
William Faulkner

"Two people are better off than one, for they can help each other succeed." Ecclesiastes 4:9 NLT

When Amy and I first started dating, we could do no wrong. If I forgot my wallet and she ended up paying for dinner, it was "cute." If she made sure her apartment was tidy before we left for a date, it was "well organized." But after saying "I do," my forgetfulness was no longer "cute," but "irresponsible." And Amy's need to be tidy was no longer "organized." She was "obsessive compulsive."

What is it that happens to us after we say those magical words, "I do?" Something begins to change. We can all attest to that fact. How do we end up being irritated by the very things that used to attract us to our loved ones? It's simple, TIME! We are now living 24 hours a day, seven days a week with each other, and we just get tired of the same things. We no longer value our differences, even though they are the same differences that we used to find attractive.

Being different from each other is what helps a couple balance their relationship. Diversity makes us stronger, not weaker, and the intent of this chapter on personality is to help each of you understand one another more intimately, and to help you see the value in your differences. This chapter helps explain why each personality is vitally important to the diverse makeup of people. Each personality has its own unique strengths, communication style, needs, and potential for balance.

The Test

Personality tests have been around for thousands of years. Psychology narrowed down all human behavior into four basic styles of being. However, typical to philosophy and psychology, the word usage in these tests has become unnecessarily complicated.

The four early descriptors of personality types are words few people actually understand. They are:

- Phlegmatic
- Sanguine
- Melancholy
- Choleric

Any clue what any of these words mean? If you said yes, (and you didn't Google them first) then you are a rare person.

Phlegmatic, you see, was one of the early descriptors for the organized and serious individual. Do you know where the term "phlegmatic" came from? Phlegm or mucus, that's right, they actually named a type of person after a bodily fluid[6]!

The Smalley system is much easier to remember, and you don't have to be offended by the categorizations. We put people in four different personality types. To describe each type, we found it best to use word pictures from the animal kingdom. Jim Brawner and Norma Smalley (our mother) were the ones who initially came up with the ideas for the animals. And of course our father and Dr. John Trent immortalized the animal personality test in their best-selling book *The Two Sides of Love*.

There is a Lion, an Otter, a Golden Retriever, and a Beaver. These types are practically self-explanatory, but you will get a more detailed description of each on the following pages.

Before you begin, take a look at the following verses:

> "Two people are better off than one, for they can help each other succeed." Ecclesiastes 4:9
> "Yes, the body has many different parts, not just one part. If the foot says, 'I am not a part of the body

---

[6] Handbook of personality : theory and research / edited by Oliver P. John, Richard W. Robins, Lawrence A. Pervin. New York : Guilford Press, 2008.

because I am not a hand,' that does not make it any less a part of the body. And if the ear says, 'I am not part of the body because I am not an eye,' would that make it any less a part of the body? If the whole body were an eye, how would you hear? Or if your whole body were an ear, how would you smell anything? But our bodies have many parts, and God has put each part just where he wants it. How strange a body would be if it had only one part!" 1 Corinthians 12:14-19

Take a moment to let each other know how good it is you both have your own personality type. Your personalities may be similar or completely different, just remember God made you for a specific reason and this even counts for your personality type.

Instructions
In the space provided, identify the degree to which the following characteristics or behaviors most accurately describe YOU at home or in the relationships you have with your loved ones.

(Personality Test on the Next Page)

Smalley Personality Assessment

0 = not at all 1 = somewhat 2 = mostly; 3 = very much

Column 1	Column 2	Column 3	Column 4
___ Likes control	___ Enthusiastic	___ Sensitive	___ Consistent
___ Confident	___ Visionary	___ Calm	___ Reserved
___ Firm	___ Energetic	___ Non-demanding	___ Practical
___ Likes challenge	___ Promoter	___ Enjoys routine	___ Factual
___ Problem solver	___ Mixes easily	___ Relational	___ Perfectionistic
___ Bold	___ Fun-loving	___ Adaptable	___ Detailed
___ Goal-driven	___ Spontaneous	___ Thoughtful	___ Inquisitive
___ Strong-willed	___ Likes new ideas	___ Patient	___ Persistent
___ Self-reliant	___ Optimistic	___ Good listener	___ Sensitive
___ Persistent	___ Takes risks	___ Loyal	___ Accurate
___ Takes charge	___ Motivator	___ Even-keeled	___ Controlled
___ Determined	___ Very verbal	___ Gives in	___ Predictable
___ Enterprising	___ Friendly	___ Indecisive	___ Orderly
___ Competitive	___ Popular	___ Dislikes change	___ Conscientious
___ Productive	___ Enjoys variety	___ Dry humor	___ Discerning
___ Purposeful	___ Group-oriented	___ Sympathetic	___ Analytical
___ Adventurous	___ Initiator	___ Nurturing	___ Precise
___ Independent	___ Inspirational	___ Tolerant	___ Scheduled
___ Action-oriented	___ Likes change	___ Peace maker	___ Deliberate
___ TOTAL	___ TOTAL	___ TOTAL	___ TOTAL

Total your scores at the bottom of each column. Your highest score is your strongest personality trait.

Plot Your Scores on the Graph

	Column 1	Column 2	Column 3	Column 4
	The Lion	The Otter	The Golden Retriever	The Beaver
60				
55				
50				
45				
40				
35				
30				
25				
20				
15				
10				
5				

Your Personality Interpretation

The Lion (Column One)

Relational Strengths: Takes charge. Problem solver. Competitive. Enjoys change. Willing to Confront.

Strengths Out of Balance: Too direct or impatient. Too busy. Cold-blooded. Impulsive or takes big risks. Insensitive to others.

Communication Style: Direct or blunt. One-way communicator. They talk, others listen.

Weakness: Not a good a listener.

Relational Needs: Personal attention and recognition for what they do. Areas where he or she can be in charge. Opportunity to solve problems. Freedom to change. Challenging activities.

Relational Balance: Add softness through tone of voice and tender touches. Become a great listener.

The Otter (Column Two) ·

Relational Strengths: Optimistic. Energetic. Motivator. Future oriented.

Strengths Out of Balance: Unrealistic or daydreamer. Impatient or overbearing. Manipulator or pushy. Avoids details or lacks follow-through.

Communication Style: Can inspire others. Optimistic or enthusiastic. One-way communicator. They talk, others listen.

Weakness: High-energy, can manipulate others.

Relational Needs: Approval. Opportunity to verbalize. Visibility. Social recognition.

Relational Balance: Be attentive to partner's needs. There is such a thing as too much optimism.

Golden Retriever (Column Three)

Relational Strengths: Warm and relational. Loyal. Enjoys routine. Peacemaker. Sensitive to other's feelings.

Strengths Out of Balance: Attracts the hurting. Missed opportunities due to inability to decide. Stays in a rut. Sacrifices own feelings for harmony. Easily hurt or holds a grudge.

Communication Style: Indirect or "beats around the bush." Two-way communicator. Great listener.

Weakness: Uses too many words or provides too many details.

Relational Needs: Emotional security. Agreeable Environment.

Relational Balance: Learn to say "NO" … establish emotional boundaries. Learn to confront when own feelings are hurt.

The Beaver (Column Four)

Relational Strengths: Accurate and precise. Quality control. Discerning. Analytical.

Strengths Out of Balance: Too critical or too strict. Too controlling. Too negative of new opportunities. Can't see the forest for the trees.

Communication Style: Factual. Two-way communicator. Great listener (in regards to details, not necessarily emotions like the Golden Retriever).

Weakness: Desire for detail and precision can frustrate others.

Relational Needs: Quality. Exact expectations.

Relational Balance: Total support is not always possible. Thorough explanation isn't everything.

Relationship Dynamic Report

Now that you have discovered who you are in the Smalley Personality System, you can choose the profile in the following pages that matches your two types. We've included some helpful tips unique to your personality combination. Feel free to read all the possible matches, but you can also simply jump to the one specific to you.

A Lion and Lion Marriage

Marital Strengths

So you're a Lion married to a Lion. The good news is that the two of you make one powerful couple! The world is at your finger-tips because you love a good challenge, nothing scares you, and you believe that anything is possible.

You also understand each other's intensity much better than any of the other personality types. You are going to be passionate, intense, and will take the success of your marriage seriously, because you want to win at having a great marriage.

Key Conflict Areas

The biggest issue for the Lion and Lion marriage is your intensity. No one ever has to guess if a Lion is upset. The two

of you probably get into epic arguments and disagreements because you are both so strong. Maybe the passion we mentioned in the strengths has turned into animosity.
You are going to struggle with not fighting about everything. You are both naturally gifted at confrontation, but this can lead to the two of you going at each other's throats from time to time.

Allowing your partner to take the lead or to have a different opinion is going to be difficult for you. Because of your strength, you can get out of balance with each other by being too dogmatic and opinionated and unable to accept another point of view.

You are both great if you happen to be on the same page, but if you disagree, that's when the conflict can get ugly.

A Lion and Otter Marriage

Marital Strengths

A Lion married to a Otter can be a truly fun dynamic for a marriage. You've got lots of energy both on the fun side of life (from the Otter) and on the accomplishment side of life (from the Lion). The two of you can utilize each other's go-for-broke attitude to accomplish things in your marriage, with your kids, and in your community.

Together, the two of you can truly conquer the world. You can be fearless and comfortable with taking risks because you are both on the risk-side of the personality scale.

Key Conflict Areas

The area you will want to watch out for is in how you communicate with each other. Unfortunately, neither of you are the best listeners. If you remember your individual personality profiles, you can both be one-way listeners, the Lion, because you are focused on solutions or building your own argument, and the Otter, because you are simply distracted or bored with the conversation.

You two need to be more deliberate about listening to each other and not getting caught up in trying to change your partner. The Lion is going to want to say, "Be more reliable" and the Otter is going to say, "But you married me...for me!" Your two personality styles are different enough that you are going to struggle trying to change each other to be more like yourself. This is not going to send a message of unity or understanding.

To the Lion, remember that your Otter partner is not going to respond to harshness or criticism like you do. Be positive and high energy when dealing with your Otter. To the Otter, try and take it easy with all the unfocused energy. Your Lion partner likes change, but change that is purposeful and strategic.

A Lion and Golden Retriever Marriage

Marital Strengths

This is one of the more common marriages we've found through our own research. Lions love Golden Retrievers and Golden Retrievers love Lions! You two fit together well, because your strengths as individuals compliment each other well. The Lion has finally found someone who likes to listen to them and also compliant and easy to get along with. The Golden Retriever has found someone with strength and focus, which makes him or her feel safe and protected.

You can bring a great balance of the hard side of love (like confrontation) by the Lion and the soft side of love (like hugs and kind words) from the Golden Retriever. You can both quite naturally teach the other person how to be a better-balanced person. You compliment each other in that way. The Lion can learn how to be softer and the Golden Retriever more willing to confront.

Key Conflict Areas

Where the two of you are going to get into trouble is by the Lion bulldozing over the Golden Retriever's feelings or needs. Because the Lion is so strong, the Golden Retriever might allow himself or herself to be controlled or dominated.

The Lion can feel unsafe because the Golden Retriever will struggle being honest about hurt feelings. This can lead to a real disconnect between the two of you. The Lion is going to be often received as "too harsh," where the Golden Retriever will be perceived as "too wimpy."

Because the two of you are on opposite sides of the personality ship, it will be a challenge to allow your partner to be authentic to their personality. You will want to change each other, probably more from the Lion wanting the Golden Retriever to toughen up, but the Golden Retriever will often shut down and think about wishing the Lion would soften up more.

To the Lion, remember your Golden Retriever partner cannot handle you dominating through intimidation. Try to approach difficult topics with a softer approach. And to the Golden Retriever, your Lion partner appreciates a more direct and honest assessment of your negative emotions. Toughen up a bit, and don't be afraid to share how you are really feeling.

A Lion and Beaver Marriage

Marital Strengths

The Lion and the Beaver...what a one-two punch! You've got all the strength and leadership of the Lion coupled with the knack for details and organization of the Beaver. You are both geared toward the hard side of love. So it's nice to be with someone who can understand you better.

You both desire success and want to do your best in anything that comes your way. You compliment each other's strengths naturally, so the learning curve to getting along is a little bit easier. A Lion/Beaver relationship is filled with strong energy and a belief from both of you to do marriage the "right way." You're leaders, and can approach everything as a team, including your family and community.

Key Conflict Areas

Where the two of you are going to get into trouble with each other is when your hard side of love gets out of balance. Your conflict can be intense, and the two of you can easily get stuck on the "facts" of an argument and ignore the feelings.

The Beaver's desire for too much detail can easily frustrate the Lion who wants to finish a task or get something accomplished. The Lion can feel held back and the Beaver can feel unsafe because of the Lion's comfort level with change.

You are both going to need to add softness to how you interact with each other. You might try giving each other a break from time to time. Everything doesn't have to be the way you want it. Learn how to serve each other better.

A Otter and Otter Marriage

Marital Strengths

All we can say is, watch out! Two wild and crazy Otters have somehow managed to follow-through together with all the wedding plans to get married; and what a fun, joyful, chaotic marriage you have.

But you are not all about fun, mostly fun, but not all fun. You two are great together because of your positive energy, ability to dream together about the future, and your love of adventure. You are both oriented toward people and wanting a good time, which adds up to a high energy relationship.

You get each other, because you both understand what makes you tick as Otters. This can help avoid some of the conflicts caused by Otters with other personality types.

Key Conflict Areas

Where you two get into trouble is when your Otter-ness gets out of balance. If you are both unbalanced, then your relationship will experience a lot of frustration over lack of follow-through, managing the details (because neither of you really want to), and staying on target in areas like budget, kids, and normal adult responsibilities.

Since neither of you are great listeners, generally, your ability to listen and communicate effectively is going to be difficult. You might often find yourselves in situations where you completely misunderstood the other, and thus missed out on trying to be helpful or doing what your partner really needed you to do. You misunderstand each other because you are too busy thinking of other things or being distracted. You don't mean to, but it could be a problem area.

The other key is learning how to be honest with each other, and not avoiding the tough conversations. Life is best experienced when you allow yourself to feel happiness and sadness. Conflict isn't bad. It is an opportunity to grow your relationship.

A Otter and Golden Retriever Marriage

Marital Strengths

This is a great combo for a couple. You've got the fun of a Otter with the sensitivity of a Golden Retriever. You are both oriented toward the soft side of love (words of affirmation, kindness, softness, etc.), and this helps you better understand each other and makes it easier to get along.

You both care about people, but for different reasons. The Otter is going to love having fun with people while the Golden Retriever is going to want to develop deep relationships with people. But the key is that you both love people, and this makes you a powerful couple when it comes to reaching out to the community.

The Golden Retriever is going to help balance the relationship by working at keeping it grounded in reality, but the Otter is going to make sure the two of you LIVE life and enjoy it. Key Conflict Areas

Where you will get into trouble is when the Golden Retriever feels overwhelmed or possibly bulldozed by the exceedingly energetic Otter. You're both very different in the way you express your energy for life; the Golden Retriever being more laid back or calm, and the Otter going for the gusto.

You might also struggle with relating to how each other wants to solve problems. You might wind up in gridlock over issues because of your differences, especially if those differences are out of balance.

Learn how to ask each other questions, because you will end up with misunderstandings due to your personality differences. When you learn to ask questions, you will find that you both want, very much, to please the other. Asking questions is the best way to tap in to your partner's built-in marriage manual. No guessing games, just simply asking each other how to repair hurt feelings or meet particular needs.

A Otter and Beaver Marriage

Marital Strengths

Now this is a match where sparks can truly fly! In our own research, Otters and Beavers are the most popular combination for married couples. The reason is because the two of you complement each other well.

You can both teach the other great things about being more balanced and healthy. You will inevitably rub off on each other, thus allowing for wonderful individual growth in maturity as people.

It is your differences that create such passionate energy toward each other. It is probably what attracted you to each other in the first place. "You complete me..." is a great line for you from the movie, *Jerry McGuire*.

Key Conflict Areas

Unfortunately it is your differences that create the most conflict. Beavers can be stressed out with their Otter partner because they feel unsafe with all the energy, optimism, and loud noises.

The Otter can feel controlled, or suppressed by the Beaver. The Beavers tendency to be focused on the possible negatives can be a true bummer for the Otter.

Also the Otter's optimism can get wiped out by the Beaver's criticism. At times, your personalities will cause stress in your relationship, because you are so different. This makes conflict and arguing over the little things more evident in your marriage than other personality combinations.

A Golden Retriever and Golden Retriever Marriage

Marital Strengths

Ok, here's the deal, the two of you couldn't be cuter and incredibly loving together. You have an easy time getting along, because you both want peace so badly. Your strengths are in serving each other, being sensitive to each other's needs, and wanting to go deep in your love for each other (and understanding of each other).

You can probably both relate to the need of routine (as long as your desired routines match). Your marriage is characterized by sensitivity and caring. You make a wonderful couple in helping others in need through community or religious volunteering.

Your home is calm and consistent; two qualities that make for an inviting home for children, friends, and family.

Key Conflict Areas

Even though you don't ever really yell at each other, you probably need to do so! You are both kind, but you are not perfect, which means you do need to engage in conflict when it happens. But you are both probably avoiders, and you thought (until this book) that not getting into conflict was a good thing, but it is not. You always bury anger and hurt alive, which means it will grow into bitterness if left unchecked.

Like the Otter/Golden Retriever marriage, the two of you must learn to be honest with each other when you are hurt or upset. This honesty will grow your marriage to places you never thought possible, but it will kill it if left unresolved.

A Golden Retriever and Beaver Marriage

Marital Strengths

Your marriage is going to be a rock to your family, community, friends, and children. A Golden Retriever and Beaver combination is the best in loyalty, direction, and consistency. You both desire a marriage worth repeating, because your marriage truly matters to you both.

When you are both at your best, you will help each other grow in areas important to making your relationship successful. The Beaver will learn sensitivity while the Golden Retriever learns better how to set boundaries.

When the Beaver wants to confront, it will be easier received than other combinations of personality types because the Beaver won't come across as flippant or thoughtless. The Golden Retriever will help the Beaver better learn how to connect with people, but without being shaming if there are any deficiencies.

Key Conflict Areas

When your personalities are out of balance, you will definitely rub each other the wrong way. The Golden Retriever might misinterpret the Beavers seriousness as not caring. The Beaver might misunderstand the Golden Retriever's overuse of words as being critical.

Facts vs feelings will be a major issue as well; the Beaver valuing facts and the Golden Retriever valuing feelings. These two issues do not mix well if entrenched in conflict. You will find yourselves getting lost in conflict because you have a hard time getting away from the facts/feelings debate.

Your expectations of each other might also cause conflict. If you put a premium on things your partner is not naturally gifted at (like you are), your disappointment with each other will cover much of your relationship. Be fair with each other, and don't expect your partner to become you.

A Beaver married to a Beaver

Marital Strengths

The Beaver and Beaver combination might not seem too exciting on the outside, but your core strengths as individuals will allow your relationship to reach amazing heights because you both desire quality so much.

Your attention to detail will give you the ability to take learning seriously. You value knowledge and skills, which are two huge qualities in keeping a relationship vibrant and on track. Being lifelong learners is a great example to everyone around you! Being two Beavers will also help the two of you appreciate the attention to detail and the premium on exact expectations. The things that turn you on relationally will work for both of you.

Key Conflict Areas

The trouble with Beavers is how hard they are on themselves...and this translates right in to your marriage and expectations toward each other. You judge yourselves harshly, but this might leak into judging each other harshly as well.

Another area of concern might be over-analyzing each other to death. If you get stuck in overthinking the stuff your partner says or does, you will miss out on seeing the big picture in your partner and marriage. This can often lead to feeling overwhelmed, which impacts the amount of hope you have in your marriage getting better.

> "God has made us what we are, and in our union with Christ Jesus he has created us for a life of good deeds, which he has already prepared for us to do." Ephesians 2:10 GNB

You may be different in your personalities, but God has created you to be unique and specifically chose your strengths to love Him and others.

"A life of good deeds" is about loving each other's unique personalities and living out the fruits of the Spirit:

> 'But the Holy Spirit produces this kind of fruit in our lives: love, joy, peace, patience, kindness, goodness, faithfulness, gentleness, and self-control. There is no law against these things!' Galatians 5:22-23

Taking it Deeper

Write down one personality trait you admire most about your partner:

_____

Why this trait?

_____

_____

_____

Pursue God Together

Read Romans 12:3, "Because of the privilege and authority God has given me, I give each of you this warning: Don't think you are better than you really are. Be honest in your evaluation of yourselves, measuring yourselves by the faith God has given us."

Why is it important to follow these words, especially when it comes to your personalities?

_____

_____

_____

_____

Key Strategy #1 - Pursue Responsibility

GOALS FOR THIS CHAPTER

You will discover:
- You are responsible for you
- No one wins in the blame game
- How your past influences you today

"If we commit ourselves to one person for life, this is not, as many people think, a rejection of freedom; rather, it demands the courage to move into all the risks of freedom, and the risk of love which is permanent; into that love which is not possession but participation."

Madeleine L'Engle

" ... Don't think you are better than you really are. Be honest in your evaluation of yourselves, measuring yourselves by the faith God has given us." Romans 12:3b

Have you ever been utterly humiliated by your partner in public? If so, how did you respond to that humiliation? Did you shut down or get fired up? (It's usually one of those two reactions!) I (Amy) got to experience humiliation at the hands of my husband back in February of 2009. I love this illustration because it is one of the times where I actually handled myself correctly (which is more than I can say for Michael) :-). Usually I am an escalator when it comes to getting angry. I tend to work my anger up like a fast moving staircase, and am often the one needing to apologize for mishandling myself during a conflict. But the dysfunction in this situation falls directly on Michael's shoulders.

It was our youngest son, David's, seventh birthday. David loves routine, and for the third year in a row, he wanted to have his birthday at a place near our house called Pump It Up. It is a great venue for kids and is filled with these awesome air-blown trampolines, slides, and obstacle courses. We downloaded Pump It Up's birthday invitations as an example for us to edit and customize to our taste.

Over the years, Michael has learned how to use graphic design programs like Photoshop and Adobe InDesign. He has often said, "When you can't hire a graphic design team, you do the graphic design work yourself." After we downloaded the invitation, Michael had the idea of making custom graphic changes to the invitation. I was thrilled by his suggestion to print the parental permission form on the back. I thought, "genius idea!" and I gave him the thumbs up to make even more changes. We talked about what we wanted added to the cards, and then he made the changes. I was quite excited about what we had done to the card! And this would be the last time I felt any kind of positive emotion about this invitation.

The very next morning was the start of a two-day Pursue Private Intensive. I had to leave early in the morning and was gone before my kids even awoke. Michael was in his office putting the finishing touches on the birthday invitation when our seven-year-old walked in and excitedly asked what he was doing. He showed him the card on the computer and David loved it! Then our son asked a question. The answer Michael gave to his question will haunt me for the rest of my days. "Daddy, did you tell them what I want for my birthday?"

Sounds like an innocent question, doesn't it? But Michael had no idea of the consequences his decision would reap in only ten short days.

Michael replied to David's question with a resounding, "Wow! I hadn't thought of that! Daddy can put whatever you want on this card. I'm designing it!" So our son asked his father, who should have known better (how many times have you said that?) to put on his birthday invitation (that was going to be seen by every single mother in David's class), "**David is requesting CASH**," in a huge banner across the top. Some of you are gasping, and some of you are wondering what the big deal is right? For those of you who know who Emily Post is, then you may pick your jaw up off the floor. But for those of you who neither know nor care about Emily Post, then you will have to stretch your brain to understand why this was a big deal to me.

I still have a hard time believing Michael didn't consider how this request might come across as inappropriate and rude. But alas, he did not. Michael printed the cards, folded them up, and handed them out to each kid in the class. It wasn't until later that day, when he was sitting under the big oak tree at our kid's school, that he wondered if it was weird to put such a request on a birthday card.

One of the moms in our son's class was sitting next to him under the tree. Michael leaned over and asked her if she had opened the invitation yet. She said no. He then asked her if it was weird to put David's request for CASH on the birthday invitation. Her response was classic, "Oh no you didn't. You didn't put 'David's wants _CASH_' on his birthday card?" He said, "Yes, Yes I did." Suddenly he was feeling a little unsure of his decision. She then asked, "Does Amy know?" He said, "No, I thought it would be cool to put that on there so David could get the really good remote control car he wants, and we wouldn't have to buy it." The mom then said to him, "If Amy doesn't know, don't tell her. She must never know."

I (Michael) don't usually endorse keeping secrets, but I did feel that keeping this secret could have real implications on my life continuing or ending (which seemed apparent by the fear this woman instilled in me!)

The party came and I (Amy) was clueless about the invitation. I did wonder why all the moms were only bringing cards as gifts. I mentioned to Michael it didn't bother me, in fact, it was quite the opposite. I was actually pretty happy that the moms did not feel obligated to bring David more gifts. I assumed that the cards were only cards. I did not yet know the cards contained

CASH! I just figured David already had enough toys and was content with no presents to eventually organize and clean.

Can you imagine my (Michael speaking again) horror at the total health of my wife! Here I was, getting prepared to be lambasted by my wife, and she pulls out this statement! I could not believe my ears. I knew Amy was loving and gracious, but this was crazy! I already felt bad for what she was about to find out, but then her attitude of graciousness at thinking no one was bringing any gifts only made my sickness even worse.

[I've said my peace, Amy can continue now.]

Okay, now back to the story....

Michael was quickly becoming aware of how much trouble his suggestion was about to get him into. And then it happened. One of the moms, who is also a good friend of ours, came right up to me with David's present. It was a nicely colored tin jar filled with coins. She was quite proud of her sarcastic moment and winked at Michael, knowing full well that she was getting him into trouble! She knew what Michael had done, and she was rubbing it in a bit. She handed me the invitation and politely said, "Michael made it so easy to shop for David this year. Look he even tells what David wants right here in this banner."

That was it. The secret was out, and I did what any wife would do in that moment. I gave the look. You know that look of "You are trouble now buddy." I playfully, yet in an "I mean business" kinda way, whacked Michael across his arm, pulled him close to my lips, and whispered, "We'll talk about this later."

I did it! I actually controlled my emotions and put them on hold until we could finish David's birthday party. Nothing is worse than ruining a party with a horrible fight. I knew this and actually made a decision to put off the discussion until we got home. I wanted to keep David's party sacred, and the reality was that I did not have to respond with anger.

We Have A Choice

As boneheaded as Michael's social faux pas was, I had a choice when it came to my response. I could have easily freaked out at the party and really let Michael have it for humiliating me in front of all of David's friends. **But I did not have to freak out**. I had a choice, and I exercised it!

Sure, Michael messed up the invitation, but losing control and handling myself in a destructive manner wasn't going to help anything. I did feel humiliated and embarrassed. And my typical response would have been to blow up. But anger does not hold the grip on me that it once had. Knowing how and when to express my feelings is something I have learned over time.

And that's the point. We all have a choice when it comes to our reactions. If you don't believe us, then perhaps Dr. Viktor Frankl can help. It is an illustration we like to give people who resist the idea of taking charge of their own reactions and emotions. Dr. Frankl was an Austrian neurologist and psychiatrist who survived the Holocaust. Early on in his imprisonment, he realized something important, he didn't have to be miserable. He wrote after surviving the Holocaust, "Everything can be taken from a man but one thing: the last of human freedoms - to choose one's attitude in any given set of circumstances, to choose one's own way."[7]

Here is the reality. There are no victims in a healthy marriage, only two people responsible for their own emotions and reactions. We are neither powerless nor out-of-control. We each contain the ability to choose when, where, and how we respond to any circumstance or situation. We are not a victim of our circumstances nor are we victims of other people. People may victimize us, but we define who we are and what we believe, by how we respond.

We aren't saying your feelings and your pain don't matter. We believe feelings and emotions are important and should be taken with great importance because they reflect the most vulnerable part of who a person is. We want feelings to be valued, but in order for them to be valued, they need to be understood in the right healthy environment.

Your partner and other people are going to continue to hurt you. We want you to know you can make the right stand and choose to respond in a productive, loving manner.

---

[7] Frankl, V. E., & Allport, G. W. (1969). Man's search for meaning: An introduction the logotherapy. Washington Square Press.

The Blame Game

When we say, "It's not my fault!" we take on the attitude of blaming. In this chapter, we want to unpack blaming and show you how it destroys the chance of a happy marriage.

> So be careful how you live. Don't live like fools, but like those who are wise. 16 Make the most of every opportunity in these evil days. 17 Don't act thoughtlessly, but understand what the Lord wants you to do. Eph. 5:15-17

I (Amy) thought marrying the son of a world famous marriage expert would mean a blissful marriage? But I couldn't have been more naive! Michael and I found ourselves at a place where death or divorce felt like an option and that was after only six months of marriage! We were miserable, and we could not see the light of day through all of our constant fighting and avoiding each other.

I would get my feelings hurt or express an unmet expectation in a harsh manner, which came across to Michael as yelling, and then Michael would stop talking altogether and leave our tiny apartment. This seesaw of emotions made life and our marriage miserable. We easily could have been one of those "starter marriages," where a young couple gets married and divorced in less than a year's time.

What was wrong with us? I would love to share all the things Michael was doing that hurt my feelings, but since I'm trying to "own" my reactions, I guess I should stick with how my reactions were hurting the marriage and contributing to the brokenness.

You see, it all started the day I was born. (I'm not kidding!) Unfortunately, I'm not perfect, and my view of everything is filtered through my family background. This includes my personality, my history, and my learned patterns of behavior. When things started to turn for the worse in our marriage, I pointed to what was different about us and viewed Michael as wrong and myself as right. When things go wrong in any marriage, it is easy to look across the kitchen table and focus on all the things our partner is doing wrong to make the marriage miserable. But the reality is we were both doing things wrong and by focusing on Michael's 'junk,' I made things worse.

I tried to justify my anger through blaming him. "I wouldn't be so angry and yell if you wouldn't..." I was basically saying, "You make me yell! I don't want to yell, but you keep messing up! You're the problem here buddy!"

Justifying and blaming our partner does not work. It actually leads to even worse feelings of bitterness and unforgiveness. The cycle of blaming does not improve our situation. It always makes it worse.

I will tell you that blaming Michael led me to feel very trapped. I was trapped in my anger because I didn't feel like I could control it. It was Michael's responsibility to do or not do... whatever... in order for me to remain calm. I convinced myself that I was a victim of Michael's unhealth. It was not my fault, but Michael's! The only problem was that the relief I felt for blaming Michael only seemed to make our marriage worse. My attitude did not help our marriage, it hurt it.

Why Blaming Doesn't Work

Blaming doesn't work because it disconnects us from each other. Blaming is a reflection of our pride, which prevents us from seeing the truth in our marriage, the truth that we are just as messed up as our partner.

We like to say there are two kinds of people in this world. Those people who are "normally dysfunctional" and those people who are "especially dysfunctional." Notice how no one is free from dysfunction? There are just different levels of dysfunction. Normal dysfunction is like you and us - normal people trying to make their way in the world and trying to do the right thing. Especially dysfunctional people are those who do the truly evil things in life.

We must take full responsibility for how we respond to people and circumstances. When we take responsibility for our actions, we are humbling ourselves, which invites relationships to grow. We called this chapter, *You Are the Foundation*, because you can create an environment for your marriage to succeed. And a healthy relationship can be built upon that strong foundation.

Perception Is Everything

In the Smalley Marriage Intensive Program workbook, we have a section titled, "Perception Is Everything." We wanted to include this here in the book because it is a powerful way to help you take responsibility for your own actions.

The perception of your life, up to this very moment, has shaped who you are, how you see things, what you feel, and why you do what you do. Our goal is to help you understand how you view your partner and the ways your past is influencing you currently.

Understanding key events from your past will help you understand what is happening today in your relationship. We want you to go through a series of questions with each other. There are four major areas you will work through in the following pages:

1. Your family of origin
1. Life altering moments
2. Your relationship history
3. Your perception of the relationship today

As you go through the upcoming questions, write down insights that come up. Pay attention to each other's responses. This will help you better understand each other. Listen to your partner with a listening ear, not a critical ear. Try not to correct his/her perceptions of the past. Saying things like, "Well that's not what your mom told me about that…" etc. will not help the other person feel understood. Most of us have gone through difficulties in our past, and we want to be understood and feel accepted. Use this as an opportunity to be an encourager. Listen for positive themes and/or positive character qualities that are revealed.

Foundation Questions

Your Family Of Origin

- What were your family dynamics growing up?
- How was love communicated?
- Who did you feel the most loved by?
- What was the biggest message you got growing up?
- What was emphasized the most in your family; education, work, play, etc.?
- How did your parents express anger?
- How did you learn to resolve conflict?
- What was the most negative thing you remember from your family?
- What was the most positive thing you learned from your family?

Write down any insights you gained from these questions.

_____

_____

_____

_____

Life Altering Moments

- Do you have an early traumatic or bad memory?
- What's your earliest favorite memory?
- Is there anything else you did not mention before that is important or meaningful that changed you in a big way?

Write down any insights you gained from these questions.

_____

_____

_____

_____

_____

Your Relationship History

- How did you meet?
- Who kissed whom first?
- How long did you date before you got engaged?
- When did you know you were in love?
- What first attracted you to each other?
- What were the character qualities that drew you in?
- What made you want to be together?

Write down any insights you gained from these questions.

_____

_____

_____

_____

_____

Your Perception Of The Relationship Now

- When do you believe things began to fall apart?
- What's good in your relationship today?
- Where do you want to be?
- What is one thing you could have done differently that probably would have made things better or not so bad?

Write down any insights you gained from these questions.

_____

_____

_____

_____

_____

Why Was This Important To Do?

It is important to go through the difficult process of disclosing your past and your partner's past so you can have a better tomorrow. By going through your own story with vulnerability and honesty, you cultivate unity, acceptance, and understanding.

By understanding someone's past, you can see the influences on their lives. What was most important to their family may or may not be the most important thing to them, but the value placed on it and how they react to that value is important to know.

Now that you have a better understanding of where your partner comes from and why you fell in love with each other, there's another exercise we like couples to do in the Smalley Marriage Intensive. It centers around the positive and negative qualities of your spouse.

Begin by making a list of all the positive qualities about your partner and write those on the page to the right above the line. Now write down some of the negative qualities about your partner, and put those below the line on the page to the right.

POSITIVE QUALITIES
NEGATIVE QUALITIES

You just wrote your beliefs about your mate. Everyone has positives and negatives. Most of the time your out-of-balance positives reveal your negatives. I, Amy, am a very passionate person. I passionately say and do things that many times are interpreted as yelling or controlling. But if you look at that quality from a positive perspective, you see it as passionate. If you look at the negative part of who I am, you would see me as controlling or angry.

Your beliefs about your spouse, based on your history and perception of their actions, play a critical role in how you respond to them. Revealing these beliefs allows you the opportunity to "re-frame" your negative thoughts as you learn to resolve conflict in a new way.

Taking it Deeper

You read at the beginning about the David birthday invitation disaster. Why would Amy take the time to cool off at the party? How does this relate to taking responsibility for your actions?

_____

_____

_____

_____

_____

Think of a time when your partner's action made you feel like you could only respond in one way. Did you still have a choice in how you responded?

_____

_____

_____

_____

_____

How does blaming negatively impact your relationship?

_____

_____

_____

_____

_____

What are a few things you could take responsibility for today?
Tell your partner what they are and how you plan on taking
responsibility for them.

_____

_____

_____

_____

_____

Pursue God Together

What stands out to you most in these verses:

> The man replied, "It was the woman you gave me who
> gave me the fruit, and I ate it." Then the Lord God
> asked the woman, "What have you done?" "The
> serpent deceived me," she replied. "That's why I ate it."
> Genesis 3:12-13

_____

_____

_____

Other words for "gently" are amiable, kindly, compassionate
and considerate. How does this verse apply to your
relationship specifically? In other words, what kind of attitude
does God expect us to have when confronting someone?

> They should **gently** teach those who oppose the truth.
> Perhaps God will change those people's hearts, and they
> will believe the truth.
> 2 Timothy 2:25

_____

_____

How does the following verse apply to personal responsibility?

> Here is a simple, rule-of-thumb guide for behavior: Ask
> yourself what you want people to do for you, then grab
> the initiative and do it for them. Add up God's Law and
> Prophets and this is what you get.
> Matthew 7:12 MSG

_____

_____

_____

Activity

Today you want to meditate specifically about possible pride in your life. Pride is a killer of responsibility and sets us up to blame others for our circumstances and feelings.

If you come to an important realization about yourself and pride, how could you add humility to your life and relationship?

One of the best ways to eliminate pride and increase humility is to serve others. What is one thing you could do for your partner today? If you can't think of anything, simply approach your partner and ask if there is something you could do for him or her.

_____

_____

_____

_____

_____

Activity

What are some things you've been blaming your partner about in your marriage or your personal life? List them below:

_____

_____

_____

_____

How can you take personal responsibility in these areas? If you feel stuck, then ask your small group or mentor to help with this activity.

_____

_____

_____

_____

Activity

Have you looked in the mirror yet and figured out what **you** need to change in your marriage (not what your partner needs to change)? If not, this is your time. We want you to think about all the areas you need to improve in your marriage that would help make your marriage stronger. List them below:

_____

_____

_____

_____

_____

This is the list you need to think about each time you want to confront your partner about something he or she needs to change. Then maybe your approach will be much softer or you might decide to keep quiet.

Fun Activity

Do something fun today. One of the most critical things you can do for your relationship is to simply go out and goof off together.

During your date, you can ask each other the following questions to help get the conversation going:

- What is your very first memory of us?
- What is your favorite memory of us so far?
- Name your favorite date we had before we got married?
- What was the best part of our wedding for you?
- What activity do you enjoy doing with me the most?
- If you could be any superhero, who would you be and why?
- Who is your real-life hero? Why?
- If you could be a movie star, would you want to be in comedies or drama?
- What was your favorite memory growing up?

How did your fun time activity go?

_____

_____

_____

_____

Chapter Journal

What have you discovered after reading and experiencing this chapter?

_____

_____

_____

_____

_____

_____

_____

_____

_____

_____

_____

Key Strategy #2 - Pursue Healthy Reactions

GOALS FOR THIS CHAPTER

You will:
- Discover why couples get into trouble
- Begin learning how to recognize your buttons
- Understand why you have to change your reactions

"Love is like the wind, you can't see it, but you can feel it."
Nicholas Sparks, *A Walk to Remember*

'Fools vent their anger, but the wise quietly hold it back.'
Proverbs 29:11

All I (Michael) wanted to do was go to a nice dinner with my wife and enjoy an Avril Lavigne concert. (I seriously debated changing the details of who we were going to see in concert so as to not lose my man card, but didn't want to lose transparency points and trust with you, so I hope I gained more trust points than lost man points!) Right as we were walking into the concert, I brought up a teaching I just attended of one of my favorite authors, which I will keep anonymous because of what I am about to write.

Before I go on, every couple goes through conflict and feels disconnected. We want to make sure, early on, you understand this principle. No relationship is perfect, no couple is just right for each other. And this includes our own relationships. We may be the teachers, but we are not perfect either. I (Michael) was on a date with Amy and things got turned upside down pretty quickly. Dates are important to keep the romance alive in your relationship. We go on dates often. Later, we will write more in-depth about how to keep dates sacred and free from conflict, but for now, I want to share how Amy and I did the opposite on this date.

I made what I thought was an observational comment, "It's funny that his writing is genius, but his voice sounds like a cross between Elmer Fudd and that annoying ex-girlfriend of Chandler on Friends… Remember the one with the horrible laugh? And he looked so nerdy. The way he dressed was straight out of the eighties." I was honestly just being silly, albeit rude, but trying to be funny. This particular author is one of my greatest heroes, one I have the utmost respect for and have read everything he has ever written. I truly was just trying to be goofy and did not mean any serious disrespect by the comment, however harshly it came out. But Amy took up an offense for him and pushed back at me with a dig. "Well you're one to talk about imperfection, it's not like you're perfect. You have things about you that could be seen as horrible or nerdy too. You aren't a good judge…"

And we were off to the races... This may happen to you too, you are out trying to have a good time and someone makes a poor comment and the other one responds with an equally poor comment. Then all of a sudden, you are both out of your minds upset about something and the night spirals out of control. The date is over and ruined before it ever has a chance to be fun.

Amy made a move to repair the damage of her comment, but before she got a sentence out, I shot out of my seat and announced she could enjoy the concert alone. It was about as mature as the teeny-boppers attending the concert! I promptly headed to my truck and sat in the front seat for the next two hours because the ticket attendant wouldn't let me back into the concert once I left.

I (Amy) didn't know what happened when he didn't come back. I thought he was just leaving to cool off, but when I didn't see him at intermission, I started thinking I might need to call a friend to pick me up. You can just imagine the scene. But fortunately, we found each other before the night got "too" out of hand.

You may not have this exact same story, but you have one similar to it. All relationships experience conflict. It is natural, necessary, and it actually increases the intimacy you feel for each other if you learn how to understand it and lean into it. We are trying, in this experience, to help you understand conflict. If you can understand the WHY of conflict, then you will gain control and power over it.

Understanding Buttons

When someone makes you mad, you might say they are "pushing your buttons." It's a common phrase, one that even kids use. Typically, when people use this phrase what they really mean is, "You are making me mad."

But guess what? When you say someone is pushing your buttons, they aren't "making you mad" (that's your reaction to the button pushing). But you are still correct in your statement. They ARE pushing your buttons. And it's important for you to understand what that means.

The reason I (Michael) got upset at the concert was not because Amy used my comment to bring up my imperfections. The reason I left and then withdrew to my truck for two hours was because a "button" was pushed in my heart. The button (hurtful feeling) that got pushed for me in that moment was the button of feeling judged. The second I felt judged and attacked, I took off.

I (Amy) got a button pushed as well. When he made that comment, I felt insulted for our friend. It was not right for Michael to say something so off-color about someone we know and love. My button was injustice. When that button was pushed, I reacted and took up an offense for that author and then took a shot at Michael.

Sound familiar?

When couples come to us for help, they often point to their problems and conflicts as issues over finances, kids, in-laws, or sex. They complain about surface level events (facts), just like the kind of conflict we described.

The problem is that you are not miserable because of facts like finances, kids, in-laws, or sex. You are not miserable because you married the wrong person. You are not miserable because of some "circumstance" in your relationship. The reason you are miserable is because a button is getting pushed and you are reacting in an unhealthy manner.

The problem is *your reaction* to your button getting pushed, not your circumstances. Start controlling your reactions, and things can get better. Try controlling your circumstances or even your mate's comments, and things will probably get worse. This is extremely important. The more you try to control things that are out of your control, the more miserable you will feel. So stop wasting perfectly good energy trying to control what you cannot. Instead, start working on what you can control, your reactions, and wait to see what happens. Your life, relationships, and overall satisfaction will increase because you will be making better decisions with how you treat yourself and those around you. It is an amazing thing to see how people respond to being treated well.

And as you will see, when your button gets pushed, you tend to push your partner's button in return, and it creates this negative cycle of unhealth. We will get to this cycle in a moment. First, here are some of the more common buttons that get pushed for husbands and wives (but by no means is this list exhaustive):

- feeling disconnected
- feeling controlled
- feeling like a failure
- feeling invalidated
- feeling rejected
- feeling devalued
- feeling abandoned
- feeling humiliated
- feeling embarrassed
- feeling judged
- feeling unimportant
- feeling injustice
- feeling disrespected

These buttons are the most common. Which ones do you relate to most? Men have a tendency to feel controlled or like a failure many times because they are hardwired to be doers. It is our opinion that men were created to do and "the doing" aspect of who they are gets invalidated many times in a conflict. They might feel like a failure, controlled, not good enough, or unappreciated. Women are more relationship oriented, so their buttons are usually based on more relational aspects like feeling rejected, abandoned, disconnected, or devalued.

We told you earlier that you are not mad because of the surface things like your partner forgetting to take out the trash; that is simply a circumstance. You are mad because when you found out your partner forgot to take out the trash, the button of feeling unimportant got pushed. Your anger is about feeling unimportant and not about taking the trash out.

Many of you are thinking right now, "But it is about the trash! Just take out the stinking trash, and I wouldn't feel upset or unimportant!" Unfortunately, this is not true. Because if it is not the trash, then it will be something else. Working too late, not sticking up for her, etc., etc., etc. It will always be some circumstance.

If you want a deeper, more intimate relationship, then stop thinking about circumstances and start paying attention to the buttons you are pushing. Because it is about the buttons. And buttons are worth talking about because you show you care when you value how someone is feeling.

Circumstances are facts, and facts can be argued. If you do not believe us, then take a walk down your own memory lane. Think back to your own arguments. How many hours have the two of you wasted arguing about facts? Too many!

Factual discussions create an environment of a courtroom, and is a courtroom the kind of relationship you are trying to create? We think not. The day we learned to stop focusing on facts and started focusing on feelings is the day our relationship turned around.

The Conflict Dance

This is an unending, cause-and-reaction nightmare for couples that is often the reason couples divorce. Take a look at the following example of the dance.

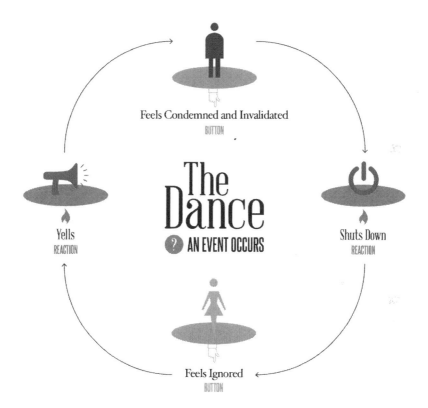

Notice how our reaction to the event ends up pushing each other's buttons each time we react, causing us to spiral out of control? It creates a never-ending cycle of hurt and bitterness, which left unchecked, will lead to divorce.

To make sure you fully understand how to identify which of your buttons causes the Conflict Dance, we want you to work through this helpful exercise developed by my (Michael) brother, Dr. Greg Smalley. Be sure to work through each step to help you identify your buttons.

Identifying Your Buttons Exercise

Step One

Identify the conflict: Identify a recent conflict, argument, or negative situation with your partner —something that really "pushed your buttons" or upset you. Think about how you were feeling and how you wished the person would not say or do the things that upset you. You might have thought something like:

"If only you would stop saying or doing _____, I would not be so upset."

Write down a short description of the conflict:

_____

_____

_____

_____

Step Two

Identify your feelings (buttons). How did you feel in response to this conflict or situation? How did that conflict or negative situation make you feel? Check all that apply—but "star" the most important feelings:

✔ or *	"As a result of the conflict, I felt…"	What That Feeling Sounds Like
	Rejected	The other person doesn't want me or need me; I am not necessary in this relationship; I feel unwanted.
	Abandoned	The other person will ultimately leave me; I will be left alone to care for myself; the other person won't be committed to me for life.
	Disconnected	We will become emotionally detached or separated; I will feel cut off from the other person.
	Like a failure	I am not successful at being a husband/ wife, friend, parent, coworker; I will not perform right or correctly; I will not live up to expectations; I am not good enough.
	Helpless	I cannot do anything to change the other person or my situation; I do not possess the power, resources, capacity, or ability to get what I want; I will feel controlled by the other person.
	Defective	Something is wrong with me; I'm the problem.

	Inadequate	I am not capable; I am incompetent.
	Inferior	Everyone else is better than I am; I am less valuable or important than others.
	Invalidated	Who I am, what I think, what I do, or how I feel is not valued.
	Unloved	The other person doesn't care about me; my relationship lacks warm attachment, admiration, enthusiasm, or devotion.
	Dissatisfied	I will not experience satisfaction in the relationship; I will not feel joy or excitement about the relationship.
	Cheated	The other person will take advantage of me; the person will withhold something I need; I won't get what I want.
	Worthless	I am useless; I have no value to the other person.
	Unaccepted	I am never able to meet the other person's expectations; I am not good enough.
	Judged	I am always being unfairly judged; the other person forms faulty or negative opinions about me; I am always being evaluated; the other person does not approve of me.
	Humiliated	The relationship is extremely destructive to my self-respect or dignity.
	Ignored	The other person will not pay attention to me; I feel neglected.

	Insignificant	I am irrelevant in the relationship; the other person does not see me as an important part of our relationship.
	Other	

Step Three

Identify your reactions: What do you do when you feel [insert the most important feeling from step #2]?

_____ (i.e. rejected, disrespected, etc.)

How do you react when you feel that way? Identify your common verbal or physical reactions to deal with that feeling. Check all that apply—**but "star" the most important reactions**:

✔ or *	Reaction	Explanation
	Withdrawal	You avoid others or alienate yourself without resolution; you sulk or use the silent treatment.
	Escalation	Your emotions spiral out of control; you argue, raise your voice, fly into a rage.
	Try harder	You try to do more to earn others' love and care.

	Negative beliefs	You believe the other person is far worse than is really the case; you see the other person in a negative light or attribute negative motives to him or her.
	Blaming	You place responsibility on others, not accepting fault; you're convinced the problem is the other person's fault.
	Exaggeration	You make overstatements or enlarge your words beyond bounds or the truth.
	Tantrums	You have a fit of bad temper.
	Denial	You refuse to admit the truth or reality.
	Invalidation	You devalue the other person; you do not appreciate what he or she feels or thinks or does.
	Defensiveness	Instead of listening, you defend yourself by providing an explanation.
	Clinginess	You develop a strong emotional attachment to or dependence upon the other person.
	Passive–aggression	You display negative emotions, resentment, and aggression in passive ways, such as procrastination and stubbornness.
	Acting out	You engage in negative behaviors like drug or alcohol abuse, extra-marital affairs, excessive shopping or spending, or overeating.
	Fix-it mode	You focus almost exclusively on what is needed to solve the problem.

	Complaining	You express unhappiness or make accusations; you criticize, creating a list of the other person's faults.
	Manipulation	You control the other person for your own advantage; you try to get him or her to do what you want.

Step Four

Look at the items you starred in response to step #2. List the three or four main feelings. These are your core buttons:

Main button #1 _____

Main button #2 _____

Main button #3 _____

Remember that most core buttons are related to two main primary fears:

1. The fear of being controlled (losing influence or power over others)
4. The fear of being disconnected (separation from people and being alone)

More men fear losing power or being controlled, and more women fear being disconnected from relationships with others.

Step Five

Look at the items you starred in response to step four. List your three or four main reactions when someone pushes your main button.

Reaction #1 _____

Reaction #2 _____

Reaction #3 _____

Your responses to these exercises should help you understand your part of the Conflict Dance, including your main button and your reaction. Remember, it's common for your reactions to push the main button of the other person in the conflict.

If the other person can figure out his or her core buttons and reactions, you will clearly see the unique Conflict Dance the two of you are doing. But even if the other person isn't able to be involved in the process of discovering his or her part of the Conflict Dance, you can take steps to stop the dance, as you will learn through the rest of this book.

Now you have a much better understanding of your buttons and how to identify them in a conflict. And just as it is important to know your buttons, you need to start being aware of how you react when your buttons get pushed. Your reaction matters when it comes to stopping the Conflict Dance. This is important to understand - dysfunctional or poor reactions are the primary contributing factors of divorce. Let's explore those now.

The 4 Risk Factors of Divorce

You do not need to worry about getting rid of your buttons. In fact, you can't get rid of them. You're human. You're going to get your feelings hurt from time to time. But you can do something about the way you react.

The four most common reactions are as follows:

1. Escalate

When your buttons get pushed, you go on the defensive, "freak out," or yell. When you escalate, you have a quick temper and get aggressive with your speech. It is damaging because things are said and done which can never be taken back. The conversation rises, like an escalator, to levels where hurt is compounded.

2. Avoid/Withdraw

When your buttons get pushed, you turn and walk away to avoid conflict. You recoil at the idea of conflict, so you escape from it, hoping the conflict will somehow magically disappear. But what it does is feed negativity and bitterness. Avoiding doesn't mean hurt or anger goes away. It just means you buried it alive. Not resolving hurt leads to a slow fade of connection and intimacy.

3. Belittle or Dishonor

When your buttons get pushed, you get nasty and throw out mean names or hurtful statements. Your goal is to tear down your partner with any word or statement that comes to mind. It is an undermining of the person's character or feelings.

4. Negative Belief

When your buttons get pushed, you become judgmental and view your partner's intentions or words as negative, or even falsely negative. In other words, you view your partner in a negative light. You may feel like you are walking on eggshells. Nothing you do or say is received in a positive manner. This is the big HOPE killer. Your partner ends up saying, "Why does it matter? Nothing I do is right, so I might as well give up."

These four reactions are also (not surprisingly) the four risk factors for divorce. You have to view them as unacceptable reactions. You can no longer claim ignorance. You are officially enlightened! You have learned the truth. We aren't saying you'll never react in any of these ways again, but we are saying you have to quickly identify when you are doing one or more of them, and stop immediately.

If you want your relationship to improve, then you are going to have to take responsibility for how you respond to your buttons getting pushed. You can do it. You already know how miserable it is to get stuck in the Conflict Dance. No one likes that dance!

You are learning a new dance, the love dance, which you will learn more about in key strategy number six. A dance where you can enjoy each other, and spend quality time together free from conflict, instead of sitting in your truck for two hours while your wife sits alone at an Avril Lavigne concert.

How did our conflict end that night? It may have taken hours, more hours than it should have, but eventually Amy returned to the truck (she did need a ride home eventually), and I (Michael) had enough time to cool off and realize what button had been pushed, and frankly, what button I pushed in Amy.

The best part in teaching relationship stuff to couples, is we get to use it ourselves, and it really does work. When I saw Amy walking toward the truck, I got out, and took responsibility for my part. An amazing thing happened when I did the right thing. Before I could finish apologizing for my part, she was apologizing for her part. I acknowledged that my comments could be seen as hurtful judgments against that person, and I understood why she might feel hurt and want to take up for that person. Amy took ownership of her 'negative in return' comments, and she acknowledged my intentions were not intentionally hurtful toward the person.

We knew what was going to get our relationship back on track, and so we both took charge and did it. Keeping your relationship on track and moving in a positive direction of growth and intimacy is our goal.

We went from a miserable, button-pushing conflict dance to a reconnecting love dance by simply taking responsibility for our actions. This entire experience is designed specifically to help give you dynamic tools to get unstuck and off the conflict dance, thereby allowing you to move on to the love dance. The foundation of a healthy relationship is when each partner takes personal responsibility for their actions, and has a heightened understanding of which of their partner's buttons they have pushed.

Creating a Love Dance

I've (Roger) seen the look before. Standing quietly in the corner of our student building was a dad. His shoulders slumped, one hand in the pocket of his jeans and a gaze of desperation. He was overwhelmed. I might not be the best at reading emotions initially, but even I immediately understood he was worried. I introduced myself as the Marriage Pastor. He wasted no time in asking me a question, "I've been meaning to talk with you. What can I do to save my marriage?"

If you have ever asked this question yourself, then you know how JR was feeling. The sense of hopelessness his marriage was not going to survive his mistakes. Of course his question could not be addressed standing in the corner of the student building, so I invited JR out to lunch where he shared openly about the specific things he'd done to damage his marriage.

"Here's the good news," I said to JR after listening to his story. I wish you could have seen his face! His look screamed, "Good news! After all the things I just shared with you! Good news!" Yes. The good news is even though his wife was wounded and they were separated, she wanted to be loved. It is in our nature to crave being loved. When we learn how to do a love dance, closed hearts spring back open to love again!

I invited JR to our Pursue Oneness marriage class. If he was going to win back the heart of his wife, he needed to learn how to dance properly. "Now whatever you do, don't try and force your wife to come with you to the class," I told him, "Just let her know you signed up and will be attending." He went home and registered online for the class. His wife was curious about how the lunch went with me but then she saw what was on the screen of his computer. She'd never experienced her husband being interested in anything that could help their relationship. Frankly, she did not know how to feel about it.

After the first class, JR returned home energized about the hope he felt in restoring his marriage. His enthusiasm was infectious! His wife, Dee, now wanted to attend the next week's class. She wanted to know what her husband was learning and why his attitude toward her seemed to be changing.

The class ended up being good for JR and Dee, but they were still not feeling connected. They were committed, but they wanted romance and passion in their relationship. The problem was, neither of them understood how to meet each other's needs in a significant way. They were two completely different personalities. JR an Otter and Dee a Beaver.

JR's attempts to start loving his wife were being met with rejection. His heartfelt desire to love her fell flat. They were starting to feel discouraged again, but then we realized something together. JR kept trying to show Dee love in ways that would be meaningful to him.

This is why we developed the Love Dance! It is a way for you to discover each other's needs and most heartfelt desires. Have you ever watched, So You Think You Can Dance? It's a show featuring the best dancers in the world competing to find out who's the best. To make it onto the show they have to go in front of three judges. If they are good enough, they get invited to the next stage where they compete .

Each dancer has their own style ranging from hip-hop to ballroom dancing. The fun part of the show is watching dancers perform styles different from their own. The hip-hop expert performing the Argentina Tango is great television because it can be painful to watch them fail at something they never practiced. They are clumsy, out of sync and clearly out of their comfort zone.

You want passion and connection in your relationship, but you don't know how to dance. You feel clumsy when trying to love your spouse well, just like the dancers on So You Think You Can Dance when performing outside of their expertise. The passion is obvious when they dance in their preferred style. They make it look effortless, almost as if floating above the dance floor. It is beautiful to watch.

The Love Dance is a tool to help you discover your dance. Your relationship has its own dance, and when you discover it, passion and connection follow. JR and Dee were like two blind-folded dancers trying to figure out their style.

JR and Dee found their love dance, which you are about to do. I asked Dee an important question, "What do you want to feel in your marriage from JR?" Without hesitation she said, "EFFORT." She wanted to feel pursued above all his other interests. She wanted to know JR valued her more than anything else. But there was a critical follow-up question I had to ask, "Would you be open to sharing four ways JR could show you effort?" Her answer would become JR's roadmap back to passion and connection:

1. Go to my favorite coffee café one time a week to discuss our schedules
2. Schedule a weekly date night
3. Take over doing the dishes after dinner
4. Hold my hand in public

Next, JR was asked the same questions. He shared how he wanted to feel appreciated. His answer and roadmap for Dee was:

1. Verbal affirmation
2. Give him 20 minutes to unwind after coming home from work
3. Ride our bikes together
4. Be present and not be on the phone while spending time together

The Sunday following our meeting, JR and Dee approached me at church. Their faces told me the story. The lost and desperate gaze from JR was replaced by a huge smile and eyes sparkling with a new hope. Dee was walking alongside her husband who was holding her hand in public. It had been the best week of their marriage. Dee smiled as she told me, "We have hope again."

If you want things to be different. If you want to build a better relationship. It's time to do a Love Dance! The rest of this book is about changing how you react and creating a love dance by meeting and understanding each other's needs.

Take a few minutes and fill out your new Love Dance. This new dance is about understanding each other's greatest need and then asking what you can do to meet the need specifically. God commanded you to love your partner more than yourself. But if you do not ask how you can meet each other's needs, you will continue struggling in loving each other.

When you ask how you can meet each other's greatest needs, you are being given a "love map". An accurate guide on effectively loving each other.

Take a few minutes to fill out the Love Dance graphic on the following page. Ask each other the two questions, "What do you want to feel in our marriage?" And "What are four ways I could meet that need?"

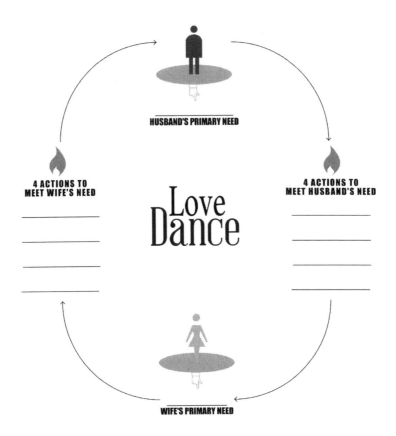

HUSBAND'S PRIMARY NEED

4 ACTIONS TO
MEET WIFE'S NEED

4 ACTIONS TO
MEET HUSBAND'S NEED

Love
Dance

WIFE'S PRIMARY NEED

First ask each other:

"What do you want to feel in our marriage?" (You can look at the four column list of possible feelings/needs to the right.)

Follow up the first question with:

"What are four ways I could meet your need?"

The following are possible feelings/needs you could use for the first question and to put on the graph to the left:

Loved	Pursued	Intimacy	Joy
Cherished	Desired	Commitment	Valued
Honor	Priority	Worthy	Treasured
Connected	Important	Accepted	Needed
Safe	Respect	Happy	Pampered
Understood	Appreciated	Fun	

Taking it Deeper

In your own words, explain what "buttons" are:

_____

_____

_____

What are the most common buttons for men and women?

For Men   For Women

_____   _____

_____   _____

_____   _____

In the past, what have you focused on more during conflict (mark your answer with an "x")?

___ Facts or ___ Feelings

How have your conversations in the past gone when you focused on facts?

_____

_____

You learned in this chapter how important it is to get off the facts and on to the feelings. Write down one or two ways you are going to begin focusing on feelings in the future.

_____

_____

_____

_____

Pursue God Together

When you are in the dark, confused and don't understand what is happening things feel more intense and scary. It's why enlightenment is important. Knowledge helps squelch the fear!

> When I refused to confess my sin, I was weak and miserable, and I groaned all day long. Psalms 32:3

Our poor reactions (escalating, avoiding, dishonoring and negative beliefs) to buttons being pushed is a product of the fall. Remember, conflict is not the problem, the problem is our poor reactions. Please take some time to confess your poor reactions (or sins) to your buttons getting pushed. Focus on your own reactions and not the ones of your partner. You might pray something like:

> Lord, forgive me for my dishonoring reaction of avoiding conflict when my feelings are hurt. I confess that avoidance is not what you desire. Give me the strength to respond in a loving way that honors you and _____ (your partner's name). Amen

Read the following scripture:

> But Jesus said, "Not everyone is mature enough to live
> a married life. It requires a certain aptitude and grace...
> But if you're capable of growing into the largeness of
> marriage, do it." Matthew 19:11-12 MSG

What does maturity look like, from a biblical perspective?
Look up the following scriptures to get an idea:
Matthew 5:23–25; Matthew 5:38–42; Matthew 5:44–46;
Matthew 18:21–22; Matthew 20:26–28.

Write down in the blanks below a 1-3 word description of what
maturity looks like based on the scripture references.

Maturity is _____ Matthew 5:23-25

Maturity is _____ Matthew 5:38–42

Maturity is _____ Matthew 5:44–46

Maturity is _____ Matthew 18:21–22

Maturity is _____ Matthew 20:26–28

Activity

Write down your buttons, the ones you identify with most often when conflict arises in your relationship:

1. _____

2. _____

3. _____

4. _____

5. _____

Think about a recent conflict and circle the above button that you believe was triggered during that conflict.

On the next page, we want you to fill in your own Conflict Dance.

Activity

Now, think about what you've learned so far in this chapter...think about how you responded when that button was pushed...how could you respond differently the next time that button gets pushed? For example, you might write down:

"Instead of escalating, I could take a timeout."
"Instead of shutting down, I could own my part."

_____

_____

_____

_____

_____

Activity

Share your buttons with your partner. This is important because you need to know each other's buttons so you can better understand each other, especially when you're upset. Keep in mind, these tools can be used as a weapon against each other as well, so please be gentle with each other with the knowledge you are gaining.

_____

_____

_____

_____

_____

Activity

We want you to spend some time in quiet meditation. Take about five minutes and ask yourself how you could begin changing your reactions when a button gets pushed. Write your thoughts down below.

_____

_____

_____

_____

_____

_____

Prayer

> Dear Jesus, I'm learning a lot about myself and how my reactions have hurt _____ (partner's name). I ask for your divine healing of my heart and for your Holy Spirit to guide my words and actions when I'm upset. Let my every thought, word and action glorify you and honor _____ (partner's name). Amen

Fun Activity

Do something fun today. Use of the following conversation starters to help get the discussion going:

- Name the sweetest thing I've ever done for you.
- What do you miss most about our life together before we had kids?
- If you could be a person in the Bible, who would you be (it can't be Jesus)? Why?
- What are you currently dreaming about your life? What is stopping you from achieving your dream?
- Describe your dream vacation.
- Describe how you see us living when we retire. Where do you want to live? What activities would we do together?
- How do you feel most loved by me?
- If you could go on a dream trip with your friends, where and what would you do?
- When you get to heaven, what will be your first question you will ask God?
- So far, what has been your proudest moment? Why?

How did your fun time activity go?

_____

_____

_____

Chapter Journal

What have you discovered after reading and experiencing this chapter?

_____

_____

_____

_____

_____

_____

_____

_____

_____

_____

Key Strategy #3 - Pursue Validation

GOALS FOR THIS CHAPTER

You Will:
- Learn what it means to validate someone
- Discover six primary ways to validate your partner and keep conflict healthy
- Identify roadblocks to validation that lead to unhealthy conflict

"And in the end, the love you take is equal to the love you make."
                    Paul McCartney

'If I gave everything I have to the poor and even sacrificed my body, I could boast about it; but if I didn't love others, I would have gained nothing.' 1 Corinthians 13:3

You want a forever kind of relationship. The question is, are you willing to do what it takes to create the environment necessary to reach forever? Being in love and experiencing the happiness you deserve comes to those who do what it takes and are obedient to the commands of Jesus.

One of the commands of Jesus helps set the tone for what it takes to accomplish this third strategy:

> "Do to others whatever you would like them to do to you. This is the essence of all that is taught in the law and the prophets." Matthew 7:12

Your ability to validate each other's feelings is a major factor in determining your level of happiness, satisfaction, and life-long commitment with each other. Validating is really living out Matthew 7:12! You know how you want to be treated, so go ahead and grab the initiative and do it for your partner!

Perhaps the best video we've ever seen on the topic of validation is the incredibly popular YouTube hit, "It's Not About the Nail," directed by Jason Headley. He does a brilliant job portraying the differences between men and women when it comes to communicating and trying to understand each other over an issue. We truly love the video because it highlights the massive hang-up most people have with validating. You can watch it now here:

http://youtu.be/-4EDhdAHrOg

As hard as it might be to believe, it actually isn't about the nail...at least when it comes to your actual relationship and not a literal nail sticking out of your head! If you want to be happy and last a lifetime, your ability to validate each other's feelings and needs is paramount. You have already learned that when your partner is upset, you know it's not about the facts of the situation, it's about a button. When you don't have to worry about the facts, and can focus on the feelings, validation becomes dramatically easier.

Validating someone's feelings is first accepting someone's feelings and then acknowledging the other person's unique identity and individuality. Validation says, "You are more important to me than proving myself right or proving you wrong."

Dr. Karyn Hall defines validation this way, "Validation is the recognition and acceptance of another person's thoughts, feelings, sensations, and behaviors as understandable."[8] The keyword in her definition is "understandable". There is a certain amount of empathy involved when you are validating someone. You aren't just being a robot repeating back what the person is saying or feeling. You are trying to empathize/ understand their feelings when validating.

Validation is NOT sympathy, however. Sympathy is feeling pity toward the person. You are not understanding or empathizing, but rather taking on a "I am better than you attitude".

We found some great examples of validating in communication at the DBT Self-Help website.[9] They organize validation into

8 Understanding Validation: A Way to Communicate Acceptance (Psychology Today)

9 http://www.dbtselfhelp.com/html/validation.html

six levels. It's important to note each level is a good way to validate someone. Level one is the most basic way and level six is the most heartfelt way, or the deepest way to validate someone's feelings. But each of the following six levels of validation are good.

Level One

Overall show interest in the other person (through verbal, nonverbal cues), show that you are paying attention (nodding, eye contact, etc.)

Ask questions - "What then?" Give prompts - "Tell me more," "Uh-huh."

Level Two

Use accurate reflection - "So you're frustrated because your son hasn't picked up his room."

Summarize what the person is sharing, then ask - "Is that right?"

Take a nonjudgmental stance toward the person, be matter-of-fact, have an "of course" attitude.

Example: "My therapist doesn't like me."

Validation: "You are feeling really certain she hates you." Note that you don't have to actually agree with the person about their perceptions.

Level Three

Try to "read" a person's behavior, imagine what they could be feeling, thinking, or wishing for. It feels good when someone takes the time to think about our life experiences. Remember to check for accuracy. It is best not to make assumptions.

Example: Perhaps your spouse is looking down, having difficulty looking you in the eyes. Clearly what he/she is saying is difficult.

Validation: "It looks like this is really hard for you to say, is that right?"

Level Four

Validate the person's behavior in terms of causes like past or present events, even when it may be triggered based on dysfunctional association.

*Validate feelings like, "Since your new boss reminds you of your last one, I can see why you'd be scared to meet with her," or "Since you have had panic attacks on the bus, you're scared to ride one now."

Level Five

Communicate that the person's behavior is reasonable, meaningful, and effective.

Validate feelings like, "It seems very normal to be nervous before a job interview - that sure makes sense to me," or "It sounds like you were very clear and direct with your doctor."

Level Six

Treat the person as valid - not patronizing or condescending. Recognize the person as they are with strengths and limitations. Give the person equal status, equal respect.

Be genuine with the person about your reactions to them and about yourself.

Believe in the other person while seeing their struggles and pain.

Example: Your spouse has just shared with you how he has felt controlled over the years when it comes to how he dresses for work. The buttons he shared are feeling controlled and belittled for how he dresses.

Validation: You might want to say something like, "I completely get how I've come across controlling over how you dress. That would be really hard to take for so many years. I

can imagine it has made you also feel like I don't approve of you as well. Would that be accurate?"
Each of these levels of validation is an important skill for building and maintaining relationships with others.

Notice with each level, you increase in your communication of empathy toward the person. The reason validation is important in a relationship is that each of us desires to be heard and understood. When we feel heard and understood, it helps us to relax in the relationship, the moment, and the conversation.

There are no "buts" or "howevers" in validating. You allow the person to feel how they want to feel- give them space so they can change their own feelings. It works because you put your feelings aside and focus on honoring the other person's feelings.

If you don't, painful feelings that are ignored will gain strength. If your partner is upset on a scale from one to ten, (ten being the most upset) and you fail to validate when they are at a five, they are going to escalate to a level nine. You know what we are talking about because you've experienced it. Think back to a time when you felt invalidated, how did you respond? Invalidation increases the negative emotions being felt, but the good news is that validating decreases the negative emotions being experienced. It genuinely has the opposite effect of invalidating.

If your partner, on that same scale from one to ten is feeling a five, then validating helps knock the intensity of the emotion down to a three or even lower.

So what does it sound like to validate your partner? The following are some validating statements you can use with each other.

Scenario One

Situation: You unintentionally hurt your partner by something you said.

Validating Response: "I hear that what I said to you really hurt your feelings. What can I do to make it right?"

Scenario Two

Situation: You have been sarcastic toward your partner, trying to be funny, and it was not received positively.

Validating Response: "I hear you're upset by what I said, instead of being funny it sounds like I was really hurtful, is that right?"

Scenario Three

Situation: Your partner is upset about something that happened at work.

Validating Response: "Wow. Sounds like your boss really disrespected you today."

The important thing to remember when validating is to focus on the value of your partner. When you highly value each other it becomes easier to validate. You want to focus on your partner's body language, words, and expressions. In other words, you want to actively listen to what is being spoken.

Roadblocks to validation

Two of the biggest roadblocks to validation are when you think validating means admitting to being wrong or that it means having to agree with the feelings or needs of your partner. Validation **doesn't** mean you are admitting to being wrong or a jerk. It means you see how the other person could interpret, or feel about your words or actions. You are simply trying to "walk a mile" in your partner's shoes. You are going for understanding their feelings, not agreeing or disagreeing to facts.

You also do not have to agree to the feeling or needs of your partner. Validating is not coming up with solutions. Validating is trying to understand your partner. Just because you validate a need or feeling does not mean you are agreeing to a solution. Solutions are win/win solutions you reach after L.O.V.E. Talk (which is coming up ahead in a chapter).

Other common roadblocks to validating are:

Negative beliefs

"My partner is going to take advantage of me."
Negative beliefs hurt your ability to validate because you are filled with so many negative thoughts that you can't validate. Negative beliefs shape your attitude, which prevents you from being able to validate.

Critical spirit

"He doesn't deserve to be validated."

A critical spirit prevents you from validating because your words and attitude set your partner up to be defensive. It is next to impossible to feel validated by someone who is critical of you.

Resentment or Anger

"I'm sick of this relationship."

Anger is one of the major destroyers of any relationship. When you sink into bitterness or unresolved anger, you literally cut off any chance of validating your partner. It's like building a wall or vault around your ability to validate. Someone who is bitter is unable to validate. Bitterness is never an option.

Pride

"Why should I have to do that? Why can't I just be myself?"

Pursue is about changing what hasn't worked in the past. Pride does not work. Pride says to your partner, "I'm right and you're wrong." Validation does not survive in this kind of emotional environment.

Guilt

"If I validate your feelings then I was wrong, and I'm a bad person."

Instead of feeling guilty, try feeling "convicted." Sunny Shell of Faith Writers explains the difference[10]:

> *Guilt only leaves you with the revelation of an error, offense, wrong, or sin with no hope of redemption, but only with the despair of condemnation.*

> *Conviction reveals an error, offense, wrong or sin, then opens the light of truth and provides a way out of shame and condemnation, and offers forgiveness, redemption, salvation, and freedom in Jesus Christ.*

You can avoid these pitfalls or roadblocks to validation by actively engaging the love skills you are learning in this book. Knowledge is power. When you know the roadblocks, you can choose to behave differently.

---

[10] http://www.faithwriters.com/article-details.php?id=80693

The benefit of validation

When your partner, or you, feels validated, the energy to fight gets sucked out of the relationship. It is like pouring a huge bucket of water on a fire. You and your partner's emotions and needs can relax once you feel validated.

Couples get into trouble when they engage in each other's hurts. You get offended, and instead of validating, you fight back and make the conflict even worse. Validating stops the hurtful conflict dance and gives you the opportunity to have a healthy conversation where you can find win/win solutions.

Can you even imagine how much better your conversations will be moving forward when you truly validate each other? The best part of this skill is that you only have to experience it once to realize the benefit!

Validating each other also brings you closer together as a couple. When you feel validated by your partner, you can't resist moving toward each other. You become irresistible to one another because you are feeling understood and valued. Your feelings and needs matter to each other, and so you respond by drawing near to one another.

Instead of being on opposing teams and fighting each other to the death of the relationship, you find yourselves together, operating as one team. Isn't this the goal of your relationship? To be together, as one? Validation gets you both back together again. It turns a hurtful, negative moment into something positive.

We tell couples frequently that a great relationship is not based on the absence of mistakes, but rather what you do to repair the mistakes. When you blow it, and you will blow it with each other, you now have an opportunity to validate and repair the damage.

Taking it Deeper

In your own words, try and explain what you understand validating means in a relationship. It helps to put things in your own words when you are learning something new. What does validating mean to you?

_____

_____

_____

_____

_____

What are some feelings or needs you would like validated?

_____

_____

_____

What are some feelings or needs of your partner that need validating?

_____

_____

_____

You are going to refer back to these in the Activity coming up.

Pursue God Together

Anger is one of the things that will prevent you from validating each other. Read the following verse:

> Do not be quickly provoked in your spirit, for anger resides in the lap of fools. Ecclesiastes 7:9

What are some of the different ways you have been angry toward your spouse? You might think back on the four risk factors (escalate, avoid, dishonor and negative belief).

Ways I've been angry…

_____   _____

_____   _____

Take ownership of your anger and ask your partner to forgive you for the different ways you've been a fool with anger.

Validation is about understanding your partner, read Proverbs 18:2, "Fools have no interest in understanding; they only want to air their own opinions." In what ways have you gotten in trouble trying to prove your own opinion?

_____

_____

_____

Proverbs 18:13 says, "Spouting off before listening to the facts is both shameful and foolish." What are some of the different ways you "spout off" before trying to validate and hear your partner?

_____

_____

_____

How can you validate instead of the different things you listed above? In other words, how might you sound different after learning how to validate?

_____

_____

_____

Activity

Look at the list of feelings or needs **you** are wanting validated from page 145. Now sit together as a couple and work through validating those feelings and needs.

For example, you might say something like, "I guess I'm feeling disconnected at times in our relationship."

Your partner would then say, "I hear you, at times you can feel disconnected in our relationship."

Activity

Look at the list of feelings and needs **your partner** would like validated. Work through those as well. The goal is for both of you to feel validated. If you need to, look back at the six levels of validating we mentioned at the beginning of this chapter.

For example, you might say something like, "So what is a feeling you would like me to validate for you?"

Your partner might respond, "Sometimes I can feel lonely in our relationship."

You can respond, "I hear that, you really can feel lonely at times in our relationship."

Activity

Practice some of the following validating statements with each other as you each take turns sharing a feeling. These statements were found at eqi.org[11]:

- What bothers you the most about it?
- How strongly are you feeling that (on a scale of 0-10)?
- How come? How so? How's that?
- So you really felt _____? Is that close?
- So what bothered you was that _____?
- What else bothered you_____?
- How else did you feel_____?
- What would help you feel better?

Please write down how these statements worked in trying to validate each other.

_____

_____

_____

_____

---

[11] http://eqi.org/und1.htm#Understanding, Empathy and Common Experiences

Fun Activity

Do something fun today. Here are some conversation starters to help engage during your time together:

- What is your definition of a date?
- Do you like kissing or hugging more?
- What food reminds you of me?
- What movie reminds you of us?
- When did you first know you loved me?
- When did you know you wanted to kiss me?
- Who do you know that has the best marriage? Why?
- What things do I do for you that refresh you the most?
- (For him) How can I romance you this week?
- (For her) How can I show you appreciation this week?

How did your fun time activity go?

_____

_____

_____

_____

_____

Chapter Journal

What have you discovered after reading and experiencing this chapter?

_____

_____

_____

_____

_____

_____

_____

_____

_____

_____

_____

Key Strategy #4 - Pursue Unity

GOALS FOR THIS CHAPTER

You Will
- Discover the power of a timeout
- Learn how to set yourself up to have a healthy conversation
- See how understanding and managing your own emotions will help you communicate more effectively

"Assumptions are the termites of relationships."
　　　　Henry Winkler

"Love must be sincere. Hate what is evil; cling to what is good. Be devoted to one another in love. Honor one another above yourselves." Romans 12:9-10 NIV

John knew he'd crossed over the line again. It was an ugly thing to say and now his wife, Julie, was sitting on their couch in tears. He didn't understand why he always got to this place. This ugly place where he said and did things he truly didn't feel. Yet, every time, the words would come spewing out of his mouth like an Apache Attack Helicopter.

What scared John the most, this time, was that Julie didn't fight back. She didn't engage in the nastiness. She just sat there on the couch, defeated and crying. How was he going to undo this mess?

It's a question many of the couples and individuals ask when they come to a Smalley Marriage Intensive. Things are said in the heat of an argument that are hard to take back - words and accusations tearing at the fabric of their commitment.

Perhaps the greatest skill you are going to discover in this book is the skill of a timeout. We know it sounds simple. We know you might be thinking there should be something more complicated or robust if it is going to be the most important skill you learn. The truth is, however, your ability to protect your relationship from the really nasty fights rests solely on your ability to stop yourself before you've gone too far.

A timeout helps you protect your relationship from the really nasty fights. A timeout stops you from going too far with your words or actions. A timeout gives you an opportunity to collect your thoughts and do the right thing in your relationship. It's one of our most favorite skills we teach couples! Because it works!

What is your favorite sport? It could be any sport, because calling a timeout in your relationship has the same benefits that calling a timeout in a sport has. Why does a coach or player call a timeout? Usually it is because something is going wrong during the game and they want to make a correction. A timeout

in sports is used to stop the negative momentum in the game
and allow for the team to regroup and get re-energized.
Coaches use timeouts to change their strategy or to remind
their players of the game plan. Famed Alabama football coach
Nick Saban won the 2017 National Title (his 6th
championship) after taking a timeout before overtime against
Georgia. Saban gave himself time to rethink his strategy for
the game because quarterback Jalen Hurts, a seasoned National
Championship quarterback, couldn't move the ball effectively
against the powerful Georgia defense. If Saban had gotten
caught up in the moment and refused to make an adjustment at
quarterback to untested Freshman quarterback Tua
Tagovailoa...who knows what the outcome might have been.
But he used the timeout before overtime to rethink his strategy
at quarterback and he went for it. Tua stepped up and
ultimately threw the game winning touchdown pass to win the
National Championship.

You can use timeouts in the exact same way in your
relationship. A timeout can be used to calm down the situation,
collect your thoughts, regroup, and then come back together
with a much better attitude.

If you're tired of breaking each other down or having to undo
hurtful words or actions, then pay close attention to the rules of
a timeout.

What is a timeout for your relationship?
Perhaps the greatest scripture in the Bible about taking a
timeout is James 1:19, "Understand this, my dear brothers and

sisters: You must all be quick to listen, slow to speak, and slow to get angry." This is the essence of what it means to take a timeout. This is yet another verse in Scripture we need to live out by taking a timeout when we get upset. It might be the best way of protecting your relationship from the four risk factors of divorce!

Google defines a timeout as "an imposed temporary suspension of activities, especially the separation of a misbehaving child from one or more playmates as a disciplinary measure." We wanted to use this definition to make an important point. A timeout between adults is NOT a disciplinary measure. Timeouts can be an effective tool for parents to use with a misbehaving child. We are not talking about this kind of timeout.

A timeout in your relationship would be defined more like "an imposed temporary suspension of yelling and screaming at each other."

Your relationship deserves to be protected from the hurt caused in "the heat of the moment" of a conflict. Both of you must begin to realize that there is no way to have a healthy conversation when you're escalated or offended. If you think about it, you know this is true. When is the last time you had a healthy conversation when you were first upset or offended? It is practically impossible to communicate well when you're upset.

This is why a timeout is so important. It helps you gather your thoughts, and most importantly, calm down emotionally before you try and resolve conflict.

Four Steps In Taking A Healthy Timeout

Step One: Create space

Either of you can call a timeout when things get heated. It does not matter who calls the timeout, you just want to make sure it is called before things get out-of-control. You might be thinking to yourself (especially if you're an escalator), "Hey, wait a second, how is a timeout different than avoiding?" Great question!

A timeout is different than avoiding because you can't call a timeout without **also** establishing a time-in. When you call a timeout it needs to sound something like, "Hey, I am starting to get really upset, and I don't want to make things worse. Can we please have a timeout so I can calm down and get my thoughts together? Could we L.O.V.E. Talk about this in an hour?"

The last statement above is what makes a timeout different than avoiding. When you avoid someone, you simply shut down and ignore the other person. A timeout is different because you are asking for a break to help calm down *and* you set a time for coming back to talk with each other.

Creating space for each other is about calming down and actually leaving each other alone for the designated amount of time. It is not a timeout if you stay in the same room and stare each other down for an hour. You've got to give each the space to disengage from the conflict and collect your thoughts. Honor each other by leaving each other alone during the timeout.

Step Two: Identify your buttons

When your buttons get pushed, you must be quick at listening to yourself and not so much to the other person. If that sounds selfish, consider the reality. When your buttons have been pushed, you are no longer safe. There is no way you can effectively listen to the other person because your heart is closed.

Have you ever tried to listen to your partner when your heart is closed? It's impossible. We don't care how relationally competent you are, when your buttons get pushed, you cannot listen effectively until you deal with yourself.

The key is to identify your feelings, buttons, fears, and hurts— your "stuff" from the conflict. Begin by working to identify what got you upset in the first place. This is when you want to look at the list of buttons, or feelings, and choose the ones most meaningful to you in the moment. What button or buttons got pushed in the argument? Ask yourself several key questions to help get to the bottom of your buttons (feelings):

- What's going on for me right now?
- How am I feeling?
- What specific buttons got pushed?
- Where is this feeling coming from?
- What is this saying about me, or what do I believe about myself right now?

Taking responsibility for your feelings means that you let your feelings and emotions (buttons) matter. You allow yourself to go to a place of compassion for yourself. You can always validate your emotions rather than ignoring them, detaching from them, or judging them.

Be curious instead of judgmental about your feelings. Care and attend to your "stuff." Allow the feelings to have space to breathe. When you validate your own feelings, you're making it okay that you're feeling whatever. Learn to view your feelings simply as information, as the language of your heart.

Step Three: Manage your emotions

After you identify your buttons, think about what a healthy response would look like. For example, take a few deep breaths, stand up and stretch, listen to music, take a walk, pray, talk to a friend, etc. Why do we want you to do all these things? You do them to get your heart open, so you can respond (instead of react) to your partner.

Remember, our natural instinct is to "react" when our buttons get pushed, instead of "responding." Reactions, by definition, are a knee-jerk response to stimuli. It's like when someone hits your knee and your leg kicks out. Reaction mode doesn't involve conscious thought; you just react. You don't want to react because that is when you will be at your worst.

The goal here is to respond to your partner. Responding is thought out. When you respond, you do things that preserve your integrity and the relationship.

Now you want to make a list of the things you can own in the conflict. No one is perfect, so there must be something you can take ownership of during the conflict. You might ask yourself some of the following questions:

- How was my tone of voice during the argument?
- What were my nonverbals saying to my partner (i.e. was I rolling my eyes, paying attention, flailing my hands in desperation, etc.)?
- Did I stick to the current conflict, or was I bringing in things from the past?
- Was I condescending during the argument?

This is not meant to be a shaming list, but realistically, we know you are not perfect and your partner has probably figured out the same thing. What is it you could have done differently in the argument?

You are not done with the timeout until you can identify your part in the conflict. Until you can take ownership of your own mistakes, you will not be ready to have a healthy conversation. Taking ownership gives you perspective, and it helps you calm down even more. The argument is no longer just about how "bad" your partner is, but rather, how you both handled things poorly. Taking ownership encourages you to be humble.

Humility is a great attitude for having a healthy conversation. The Christian Bible Reference Site defines humility in this way:

> *People often wonder what humility means or what is the definition of humility. In the Bible, humility or humbleness is a quality of being courteously respectful of others. It is the opposite of aggressiveness, arrogance, boastfulness, and vanity. Rather than, "Me first," humility allows us to say, "No, you first, my friend." Humility is the quality that lets us go more than halfway to meet the needs of others.*

If you want to have a better conversation about things that matter, issues or events that need to be resolved, it starts by you humbling yourself and owning your junk.

Step Four: Get back together and talk

Now you are ready for a healthy conversation. We can't express enough how important taking a timeout is to better understand your buttons, issues, and owning your junk. Like we said at the beginning of this section on taking a timeout, it sets you up to protect your relationship from the nasty conflicts and prepares your heart for having a healthy conversation.

A timeout allows both of you to calm down and gain much needed clarity on your feelings and needs. When you take the time to pause and gather yourself together, you can finally have the kind of conversation that allows you to both honor each other. It's just one of the ways you can be obedient to Jesus' command to love God and love others (Matthew 22:36-40).

Taking it Deeper

In your own words, write in the space below what your definition of a timeout would be.

_____

_____

_____

_____

Ecclesiastes 7:8-9 (GNTD) says, "The end of something is better than its beginning. Patience is better than pride. Keep your temper under control; it is foolish to harbor a grudge."

How do these verses speak to timeouts?

_____

_____

_____

Below are words that could prevent you from taking a timeout.
Circle any of the words you feel might be a struggle for you:

Pride	Lazy	Criticism
Selfishness	Apathy	Ill-tempered
Ego	Facts	Avoidant
Unfair	Blaming	Negativity
Impatient	Challenged	Provoked

Why did you select the words circled above

_____

_____

_____

How can you overcome these words?

_____

_____

_____

Pursue God Together

During a timeout it is important to pray and get God's perspective about why you need a break.

> Don't worry about anything; instead, pray about everything. Tell God what you need, and thank him for all he has done. Then you will experience God's peace, which exceeds anything we can understand. His peace will guard your hearts and minds as you live in Christ Jesus. Philippians 4:6-7

What are you supposed to pray about specifically as encouraged in Philippians 4:6-7 during a timeout?

_____

_____

_____

How is this going to be different from your reactions in the past?

_____

_____

_____

Read the following verses in Ephesians:

> Always be humble and gentle. Be patient with each
> other, making allowance for each other's faults because
> of your love. Make every effort to keep yourselves
> united in the Spirit, binding yourselves together with
> peace. Ephesians 4:2-3

In what ways can you be more patient?

_____

_____

_____

What does it mean to "make allowance for each other's
faults"?

_____

_____

_____

List three ways you can "make every effort to keep your yourselves united in the Spirit":

1. _____

2. _____

3. _____

Activity

What has prevented you in the past from taking a timeout when things got heated? Did you learn any bad habits from your parents or family? What are the bad habits, and what have you learned so far in this book to help change them?

_____

_____

_____

_____

_____

_____

Activity

Think of a previous argument you've had when you didn't take a timeout. How could you have done that argument differently?

Or…thinking about that argument, what prevented you from taking the timeout?

_____

_____

_____

What could you have done differently to help stop yourself and take a timeout in that argument? If you could do it over again, what would you do differently?

_____

_____

_____

Activity

Timeouts are an effective way to protect your relationship. But what can you do during a timeout to ensure your spirit and emotions are ready to have a healthy conversation?

Activity

Ask each other for the best way you could call a timeout when things get heated. You can come up with your own phrase or method, but make sure to let each other know some of the phrases or words you definitely DON'T want to hear as well.

Best way to call a timeout:

_____

_____

_____

Things you don't want to hear:

_____

_____

_____

_____

Fun Activity

Do something fun today. Here's some conversation starters to help your time together:

- What is one area of communication that I am very good at, and one area I really need to work on?
- What can we do as a couple that can change the world?
- What do we want our marriage to look like?
- Who are some couples we admire and can learn from?
- What do they do that makes their marriage stick out?
- What are some specific actions steps we can take to grow our marriage?
- Where are some specific areas where I'm just coasting in life and in marriage?
- What will we focus on in the next 12 months of our marriage?

How did your fun time activity go?

_____

_____

_____

_____

Chapter Journal

What have you discovered after reading and experiencing this
chapter?

_____

_____

_____

_____

_____

_____

_____

_____

_____

Key Strategy #5 - Pursue Communication

GOALS FOR THIS CHAPTER

You will

- Learn how healthy conflict leads to intimacy
- Understand the healthiest structure for good communication (especially during conflict)
- Discover how to find the win-win in an argument

"A wonderful fact to reflect upon, that every human creature is constituted to be that profound secret and mystery to every other."

Charles Dickens, *A Tale of Two Cities*

"Take control of what I say, O Lord , and guard my lips."
Psalms 141:3

Marriage is tough, and it's the toughness that makes marriage so wonderful! We want to propose a question to you. "What in life, worth having, is easy to achieve?" Think about this for a moment. In virtually every area of our life, we know that in order to be great, it will take knowledge, skill, practice, and a lot of hard work. No one in their right mind thinks becoming a CEO, professional athlete, or successful entrepreneur is easy. But when it comes to our relationships, our marriages, the most

common thing we hear couples say is, "It should be easier...
why is this so hard...it is just too hard..."

Do you remember playing board games with a parent or
grandparent? Do you ever remember a game where you knew
your grandma let you win? How did the victory feel? If you
were old enough, it probably didn't feel good at all, like
something was missing from the victory. The true joy of
winning was dampened by the fact you were allowed to win. In
essence, you did not earn the victory, it was given to you,
which took all the fun away from winning. You didn't have to
work at it, the win was not earned.

Why would marriage be any different? Our original question
read, "What in life, worth having, is easy to achieve?" Our
hope for you is that you look at the difficult times ahead as an
opportunity and not a tragedy. That your eyes are focused on
loving each other through the conflict instead of being buried
by it. Because conflict is coming, no matter how wonderful
your dating life is.

Healthy Conflict Leads to Intimacy

Conflict is natural. Conflict is inevitable. Conflict adds depth to
your relationship because you are sharing differences of
opinions and needs. When you get into conflict, you are
learning about each other and presenting an opportunity to
better love each other.

There is nothing abnormal or unhealthy about getting into
conflict with your partner. Conflict is the natural progression of

an intimate relationship. Conflict is actually healthy and an important part of a balanced marriage.

Conflict is a doorway to intimacy and is a part of any significant relationship. It is a healthy thing WHEN YOU KNOW HOW TO HANDLE IT PROPERLY.

The problem with conflict is most couples don't have a clue how to resolve it. They just fight and never make up or draw closer together. But it doesn't have to be that way.

We want to shed light on how to find a win/win solution in every argument. We want you to know that you don't have to be miserable and avoid topics because they are "too sensitive." This book will give you the structure and the system to find out why you are in conflict and to gain understanding about each other on a level you may not be used to – a close and connected level.

You will learn how to utilize conflict to help your marriage rather than allowing conflict to tear your marriage apart.

Yes, you heard us correctly. Conflict in your marriage, handled well, actually leads to a more intimate relationship.

How do we spell out healthy communication?

L.O.V.E.

The heart of our communication method is expressed in these core principles:

- Listen
- Own
- Validate
- Express

This acronym, developed by Teresa Thomas, who runs the Smalley Institute Center in Dallas, teaches the same principles used at successful drive-thru restaurants across the country. Yep. You're about to learn how to increase the intimacy in your marriage by way of a fast food drive-thru! (Our methods may be unconventional, but they are proven!)

If you've successfully ordered a meal from your car at a fast food restaurant, then you have already successfully done L.O.V.E. Talk. Let us explain, using Chick-fil-A (because, well, let's just say we have a LOT of experience in the Chick-fil-A drive-thru).

"Every year Chick-fil-A spends a million dollars evaluating it's service" to keep its customers happy and returning.[12] As part of their research, they discovered that their customers really only wanted three things; to be understood, for things to come out correctly, and to have their feelings and needs validated.

---

[12] Salter, Chuck. "Chick-fil-A's Recipe for Customer Service." Fast Company. Accessed February 24, 2016. http://www.fastcompany.com/resources/customer/chickfila.html.

As crazy as it may seem, we want you to replicate the Chick-fil-A drive-thru process when conflict erupts in your relationship.

Let's walk through the process together.

L.O.V.E. Talk and the Chick-fil-A Drive Thru

What happens when you first pull up to the drive-thru at Chick-fil-A? A soothing voice (albeit somewhat crackly) comes through the speaker and says, "It's a great day at Chick-fil-A, how may I serve you?" What a great way to be greeted. It's friendly, helpful, and service oriented. What's the next thing that happens? You give your order to the voice in the box. And after your order is given, the employee repeats your order back to make sure he has understood your order correctly.

Just out of curiosity, do you ever give more input than simply your order? We mean, do you ever start telling the employee what you ordered last week at McDonalds? Do you go into a 30-minute monologue describing your first experiences at Chick-fil-A as a child and the first car you owned when you made your first order alone? Probably not, which is a good thing. Not only would all that information be irrelevant, you'd probably never get the meal you ordered because there was too much discussion about the past, as well as irrelevant information.

Or, have you ever been shamed or invalidated by a Chick-fil-A employee after giving your order? For example, have you ever ordered a Chick-fil-A sandwich, large fries, a cookies and cream milkshake, and a diet coke and then had the employee not give you the order because he felt like you were too fat to eat that meal? Could you imagine the hurt and embarrassment if an employee behaved in such a manner? It would be obnoxious, and you would probably never eat there again.

But for some reason we feel like it is totally appropriate and helpful to bring up the past and other issues when we get into conflict with our partner (or anyone else).

The reason L.O.V.E. Talk is so powerful in helping you resolve conflict is that it forces you into a system of communication that fosters understanding and validation. And just as there are two roles in the Chick-fil-A drive-thru experience (employee and customer) there are two roles you play when using L.O.V.E. Talk to resolve the conflict in your relationship.

Let's continue to explore these roles. They are important because we want you to replicate this process in your home.

The Role of the Employee

The entire job of the employee is to LISTEN and VALIDATE. Listening well is not a natural gift and has little to do with your eardrum. Being a great listener, and thus a great employee, is more about seeking understanding and validating the customer's feelings and needs. Listening involves your ears, your posture, your head, and your heart. If all these elements are not working together, then you are not going to be a good listener, and L.O.V.E. Talk will be useless.

Listening helps you understand what the conflict is about. When you learn to be a great listener, you set up your marriage to succeed. Listening is at the core of loving your partner well. When your partner feels listened to, the doorway to intimacy will fly open! When your partner feels heard and validated, no matter what has happened in the past, he/she will melt at your ability to listen. We've watched couples in our Smalley Marriage Intensive program embrace for the first time in years after they've validated and listened to each other.

Validating someone's feelings is first to accept someone's feelings and then acknowledge and accept the other person's unique identity and individuality. (You already learned this earlier in the lessons. But we want to recap it here.)

Validation says, "You are more important to me than proving myself right or proving you wrong."

EX: I understand how you could feel that way…

(There are no "buts" or "howevers" in validating. You allow the person to feel how they want to feel- give them space so they can change their own feelings. It works because you put your feelings aside and focus on honoring the other person's feelings.)

Painful feelings that are ignored will gain strength. Validation doesn't mean you are admitting to being wrong or a jerk. It means you see how the other person could interpret, or feel about, your words or actions. I can say, "It wasn't my intention to make you feel …"

When your partner, or you, feels validated, the energy to fight gets sucked out of the relationship. It is like pouring a huge bucket of water on a fire, your partner's emotions and needs can relax once she feels validated.

The Role of the Customer

The entire job of the customer is to OWN and EXPRESS. What can we do to feel understood and validated, especially when our feelings get hurt? We have to OWN our buttons and EXPRESS our needs. Check out these four easy steps to being heard and validated (by the "employee") and try them the next time you want to be understood:

1. Own your stuff
2. Then share feelings and needs
3. Do not blame, criticize or shame when you share your feelings and needs
4. Only use "I" statements one sentence at a time

We owe these rules to the guys at PREP, Inc. (Dr. Howard Markman and Dr. Scott Stanley)[13].

1. Own your stuff.

The best policy when starting off as the customer is to first take ownership of anything you did wrong in the conflict. You might not feel like you did anything wrong, but more than likely, there's something you can take ownership of in the conflict. Maybe it's your tone of voice, choice of words, timing in the conflict, etc. We promise there's something you can take ownership of, and we encourage you to do that up front. Taking ownership helps diffuse your partner and keeps them from getting defensive.

2. Share your feelings and needs.

If you really want to be heard, understood, and validated, then you cannot enter a conversation with guns blazing. It does you no good to have a stinky attitude and to "bite" into your partner with bitterness and anger. I (Michael) have posted extensively on feeling words (just enter the phrase "hot buttons" in a search engine and you'll see what I mean."). If you want to be heard, then use words like, "I'm feeling rejected," or "I felt ignored the other day." If your partner is normally dysfunctional, then we can promise you that he/she does not want you feeling these things. Normal people want to feel happy and loved and want

---

[13] https://www.prepinc.com

to love and make other people happy as well. Starting off with how you feel is always the best bet to setting up your partner to receive your hurt and be able to validate it.

Then, you can share your needs, *after* your feelings have been validated. Your needs must be simple and doable. Nothing crazy or impossible should ever be shared as a need. Telling your partner, "I have a need for you never to hurt my feelings again," would be a ridiculous request. Telling your partner, "I need us to stop yelling at each other in front of the kids," is a much better need. If your partner responds negatively to your need, then share your need with someone you trust. If they have the same reaction, then we'd suggest that you come up with a different need. If both your partner and your trusted friend have the same negative reaction to your need, you need to reevaluate.

3. Do not blame, criticize, or shame your partner.

Doesn't this one just make sense to you? Has anyone in your life ever truly responded well to being criticized or blamed? If you live on this planet, your answer is a resounding no! So keep the judgmental attitude at bay when you want to be heard and validated. There is no room in conversation for blaming, criticizing, or shaming. It just does not work.

4. Only use "I" statements one sentence at a time.

This last step is important. Never, ever, ever use the word "you" when trying to be understood and validated! This will help eliminate defensiveness, and it will force you to really think about how you word your feelings and needs. By way of example, take a look at this poor way to word your feelings or needs, "You always make me feel rejected." Notice how this kind of statement will create defensiveness, and I'd guess that some of you reading this felt defensive. Say it out loud and see how it sounds, not very good – huh? Now try this same statement just worded differently, "The other night when I was left alone, I felt rejected." This has a completely different tone and attitude.

The last step in #4 is to only use one sentence at a time. You are not allowed to go into great detail when you are trying to be understood. Just keep it simple and use one sentence at a time to describe a feeling or a need. (Just like you would at the drive-thru if you were trying to get what you needed from the employee but they didn't understand you!) What is so cool about this is that you are only going to have two or three feelings and needs per conflict. So you can get all you need to be understood and validated in only a few short sentences! This dramatically shortens the length of your conflict, which is a good thing!

There you go. Now you know what it takes to share your feelings and needs in a way that can be heard and validated. Isn't this what you really want when your feelings get hurt? Try these out the next time you want to share something with your partner.

L.O.V.E. Talk solutions

So far you've learned how Chick-fil-A can help you turn any argument in to an opportunity to grow closer together. You've learned how to listen in a way that makes your partner melt when trying to share feelings. And you've learned how to share your own feelings so your partner can understand and validate you when things have gone awry.

The final piece of the puzzle in resolving conflict is learning how to reach a win/win solution after you understand each other's feelings and needs surrounding an argument. Notice how we used the term "win/win." We do not use this term lightly because when it comes to resolving conflict in a manner that draws you closer together, a win/win option is the only option. There is no such thing as a win/loss scenario in a healthy, satisfied marriage. If one of you feels like a solution is a loss, then you both lose.

Here are three suggestions on how to find win/win solutions when the solutions do not readily make themselves obvious:

- Ask a trusted friend to act as a mediator
- Go to a pastor or marriage expert (i.e. counselor, psychologist, etc.)
- Be a servant

1. Ask a trusted friend to act as a mediator

If you have discussed an issue and both of you feel like you understand each other, but you still can not come to a win/win solution – call a friend. Do not be ashamed to ask a friend to step in and offer help in finding a win/win solution. If both of you trust this person, then allow him/her to listen to both sides and then offer a third alternative or even choose either of your ideas. Couples get stuck; this is not bad or abnormal. The problem occurs when couples refuse to seek outside help. Some conflicts do not merit professional help, so ask a friend to get involved and trust the friend to make a good decision that will benefit your marriage.

2. Go to a pastor or marriage expert (i.e. counselor, psychologist, etc.)

If the conflict you are experiencing is serious, like dealing with an affair, then seek out help from an expert. When you get stuck and can't seem to find the light of day in your conflict, get help. There are people in your community that have spent years helping couples resolve conflict. Use them as a resource to keep your marriage strong. Do not allow conflict to erode your marriage simply because you are not willing to humble yourself and ask for help.

3. Be a servant

Perhaps the greatest option is to choose to be a servant. This does not mean you act like a doormat. But sometimes the most logical and helpful solution is deciding to serve your partner's needs and to lay down your life for your partner. Step up to the plate of servanthood and boldly announce that you want to hit a home run of serving your partner. That is the kind of person people want to be married to.

Now you've been able to read and understand more deeply the heart of conflict resolution. The following page has the rules summarized for you, to fit on one page. We encourage you to print the page out, frame it, laminate it, do whatever you need to keep this page as a handy reference to hold when you are trying to L.O.V.E. Talk.

Again, we encourage you to have the one page summary available when you L.O.V.E. Talk. You can download this on our website www.smalley.cc/free-content. We will include it here, in the book, but it may be too small to read.

Simply holding that piece of paper will dramatically change the attitude and tone of your discussion. How many times in the past have you held a piece of paper in your hands when trying to resolve a conflict? That's right, most of you probably answered, "Never." Married life is about getting you to do things differently, to break poor patterns of relating to one another, and replace them with knowledge and the skills to better understand and love each other. Using the one page summary of L.O.V.E. Talk will help you follow the rules, and it will be a vehicle to keep things calm.

An example of L.O.V.E. Talk

Let's take a moment and see exactly what L.O.V.E. Talk would look like if you were in an argument over someone's inability to remember receipts. For this example, we'll assume the guy isn't remembering them and the woman wants him to.

Remember, before you sit down to L.O.V.E. Talk, you should have already taken a timeout. During the timeout, identify your buttons and needs. Now you're ready to L.O.V.E. Talk:

Woman
Thanks for coming back and L.O.V.E. talking this with me. I guess the reason I got upset this morning was that I'm feeling ignored over the remembering receipt issue. (Notice she states what buttons were pushed?)

Guy
Okay, I can hear that. You are feeling ignored about me remembering receipts. I can totally get that, because I can admit that you've been asking for months about this, and I'm still not remembering them. Anything else?

Woman
Thank you, and yes, I think I realized that when I can't reconcile the checkbook with our bank, it really makes me feel like a gigantic failure. Like I'm being given a test each month, and I have no ability to pass it.

Guy
Whoa! I know how important it is for you to perform well, you always were the better student. I hear you saying that when you can't reconcile with the bank, it truly makes you feel like you're failing. Sounds like you might even feel helpless or powerless as well, is that accurate?

Woman
[nodding her head] Absolutely, like I can't do anything about it.

Guy
Anything else?

Woman
I guess what I need is for you to figure out a way to remember receipts and get them to me.

Guy
Okay, I hear you really need me to figure out a way to remember the receipts and actually hand them to you. Is that right? Anything else?

Woman
Nope, you heard it, and I do appreciate you listening. Do you have anything to say as the customer?

Guy
I actually do. I think I feel judged and condemned when confronted about not remembering the receipts. (Now it's his turn to share his buttons.)

Woman
I get what you're saying, because I can lose it and yell. Sounds like my reaction hits buttons of being judged and condemned. Is that right?

Guy
Yes it is. I think another big one for me is that when I'm accused of not loving or caring much about our marriage, I feel pretty invalidated.

Woman
I hear you. When I start in on you, it can come across like I'm invalidating your love for me or your commitment to our marriage.

Guy
Yes, thank you for hearing that. I think my biggest need in this issue is to be approached more softly if I mess it up.

Woman
I totally get that, you need me to approach more softly if I'm feeling ignored or like a failure. Anything else?

Guy
Nope, that's pretty much all my stuff. Are you open to discussing possible solutions?

Woman
I am, what do you think could help in this issue?

Guy
Well...would it be a win for you if we just didn't worry as much about receipts?

Woman
I know that receipts aren't a big deal to you, but they really are to me. That wouldn't be a win for me. Would it be a win if we got you something that would help remind you to keep receipts? Like a larger bag or something you could carry with you?

Guy
I'm open to that. My biggest fear is that I'm simply not going to remember, and I know that isn't a good option. Probably having something on me would make a huge difference in remembering receipts, maybe something like a shoulder bag or even a backpack. I could designate a specific pocket to put the receipts in, and then you could check it when I got home from trips or supply shopping. Would that be a win for you?

Woman
Absolutely, I honestly don't care how you remember the receipts, just that you remember them. And it doesn't bother me at all to check a specific pocket. I could do that.

Guy
Okay then, why don't I go with a backpack, and I can use the front zipper pocket for receipts.

You might read this example and think it sounds ridiculous, the funny thing is...it is an actual L.O.V.E. Talk conversation we had together after about 6 months of marriage. We were miserable over my (Michael's) inability to remember receipts.

When I heard Amy share how she felt ignored and felt like a failure, my perspective about the receipts changed. To this day, I don't feel receipts are important, but Amy is highly important to me, therefore I remember them because of her and not because of the importance of receipts.

This is why you L.O.V.E. Talk, to get down to the feelings and needs. No one wants his or her partner to feel ignored or like a failure. Amy didn't want me to feel judged and condemned. **When we share feelings, we become a team again, and teams win championships!**

Taking it Deeper

How does patience play out in healthy communication? What would your communication look like if either (or both of you) were more patient with each other during an important conversation?

_____

_____

_____

What does the structure of L.O.V.E. Talk provide you when you are arguing? Why is it important to have a specific, structured way to communicate when you are trying to resolve an argument?

_____

_____

_____

_____

_____

Is L.O.V.E. Talk something we do naturally or something that must be learned?

_____

_____

_____

_____

_____

Pursue God Together

Psalms 141:3 (MSG), "Post a guard at my mouth, God, set a watch at the door of my lips."

After reading Psalms 141:3 pray the following:

> Heavenly Father, post guards at my mouth because I want to honor you and _____ (partner's name)! Never let me be complacent or careless with what I say. Allow me to speak the truth in love and to desire honoring _____ (partner's name) above all else.

Read the following verse:

> Through patience a ruler can be persuaded, and a gentle tongue can break a bone. Proverbs 25:15

La Bruyère wrote, "There is no road too long to the man who advances deliberately and without undue haste; there are no honours too distant to the man who prepares himself for them with patience."

How does the quote from La Bruyère and Proverbs 25:15 relate?

_____

_____

Once again we come to a verse that commands we do everything in our power to live in peace with each other. Romans 14:19, "Let us therefore make every effort to do what leads to peace and to mutual edification."

What are some specific ways you can put in the effort to live in peace with each other?

_____

_____

_____

_____

_____

_____

Activity

Download and install our free app, "Smalley Marriage". You can find it in any smart device app store like Apple's App Store or Google Play. It works on every platform (iOS, Android, Windows, Amazon, etc.). The L.O.V.E. Talk rules and system are included in the app. **Remember, L.O.V.E. Talk is a new skill, and it will take time to become an expert at the method.**

We've also provided a quick reference guide to the rules on the following pages. You can start by filling out the L.O.V.E Talk Preparation sheet. This helps you get organized on what you can own, your buttons, and needs.

The L.O.V.E Talk Preparation Sheet

You will want to fill out this prep sheet during a timeout. It's a great way to ensure you will honor the rules of L.O.V.E Talk . As you can see on the page to your right in the book, there are four sections you fill out: The Issue, I Own, I Feel, and I Need. Remember to stick to one issue at a time, so write a brief summary of the issue you want to L.O.V.E Talk. Then you fill out the behaviors or beliefs you can own from the conflict. Next is your chance to identify any buttons (feelings) that were pushed during the conflict. Lastly, you can write down any needs you might have.

(go to next page for L.O.V.E Talk Preparation Sheet)

L.O.V.E. Talk Prep Sheet

The Issue (the conflict you need to resolve):

_____

I Own (what can you take responsibility for, maybe behaviors like escalating, avoiding, or dishonoring):

_____

_____

Beliefs (were you defensive, judgmental, or focused on the negative):

_____

_____

I Feel (these are your buttons):

_____

_____

I Need (what specifically do you need for this issue):

_____

_____

LIST OF BUTTONS

Judged	Pathetic	Humiliated
Disconnected	Heartbroken	Abandoned
Lonely	Anxious	Unimportant
Failure	Overwhelmed	Ignored
Powerless	Threatened	Neglected
Scorned	Horrified	Condemned
Invalidated	Pressured	Unwanted
Defective	Bewildered	Danger
Inferior	Ashamed	Disliked
Rejected	Exhausted	Mistrust
Worthless	Suspicious	Despair
Disheartened	Dejected	Unhappy
Offended	Devalued	Controlled

Activity

In this activity, we want you to focus on **becoming a great employee**. This is the most important role, so you need to start practicing it right away. You don't need your partner to be involved as you're practicing being a great employee. You can do this with anyone in any circumstance where needs or feelings are being expressed.

Apply and carry out the employee rules at work, with your kids, your friends, or your neighbors. List some of the things you feel will be important for you in becoming a better employee.

In order for me to become a better Employee, I need to do the following things:

1. _____

2. _____

3. _____

4. _____

Activity

Focus on the customer rules for this activity. Circle the words on this list that seem to mean the most to you. These are probably going to be your most consistent feelings to share when playing the customer role in L.O.V.E. Talk.

Judged	Pathetic	Humiliated
Disconnected	Heartbroken	Abandoned
Lonely	Anxious	Unimportant
Failure	Overwhelmed	Ignored
Powerless	Threatened	Neglected
Scorned	Horrified	Condemned
Invalidated	Pressured	Unwanted
Defective	Bewildered	Danger
Inferior	Ashamed	Disliked
Rejected	Exhausted	Mistrust
Worthless	Suspicious	Despair
Disheartened	Dejected	Unhappy
Offended	Devalued	Controlled

Activity

Sit down with your partner and practice L.O.V.E. Talk with each other. Start off with something insignificant at first, like describing a great date night. This will allow you to safely learn the method so you won't be tempted to get into a major discussion. You don't want to start off with a hard or extremely hurtful topic. In fact, if you do have a major hurt or unresolved conflict, you might want to consider having a third party mediate your L.O.V.E. Talk with each other. This can be a pastor, friend, small group leader, or therapist.

If you find your relationship getting stuck trying to L.O.V.E. Talk, you might also consider attending a Smalley Marriage Intensive where you can meet one-on-one with a coach. We have Smalley Institute Centers located around the country for your convenience. Just go to the web at www.smalleyinstitute.com to find a location nearest you. You can also speak with one of our Intensive Consultants Monday through Friday from 9am to 5pm CST by calling 800-975-8748.

Fun Activity

Do something fun today. Here's a list of different conversation starters to help you both keep things interesting:

- Would you rather fail or never try?
- Would you rather be stuck on an island alone or with someone who talks non-stop?
- Would you rather have more money or more time?
- Would you rather have a cook or a maid?
- Would you rather have nosy neighbors or noisy neighbors?
- Would you rather have mind-blowing sex once a month or mediocre sex once a week?
- Would you rather fight all the time but have great makeup sex or never fight and have mediocre sex?
- Would you rather travel the world or travel just the 50 states?
- Would you rather have a destination vacation at Bora Bora sunbathing in the sun or at the Swiss Alps snow skiing?

How did your fun time activity go?

_____

_____

_____

Chapter Journal

What have you discovered after reading and experiencing this chapter?

_____

_____

_____

_____

_____

_____

_____

_____

_____

_____

Key Strategy #6 - Pursue Attraction

GOALS FOR THIS CHAPTER

You Will:

- Discover how to behave in a way that makes you irresistible
- Learn the four key ways to become a love magnet
- Apply the skill of serving to your relationship

"Everybody can be great...because anybody can serve. You don't have to have a college degree to serve. You don't have to make your subject and verb agree to serve. You only need a heart full of grace. A soul generated by love."
        Martin Luther King Jr.

"Always be humble and gentle. Be patient with each other, making allowance for each other's faults because of your love. Make every effort to keep yourselves united in the Spirit, binding yourselves together with peace." Ephesians 4:2-3

They hadn't touched each other for close to nine years! No hand holding, hugging, pats on the back, back rubs, or sex...for nine years! They were sitting on opposite ends of the couch, it looked as if they couldn't get far enough away from each other. They might as well have been on opposite sides of the Grand Canyon. How they were still married is a miracle in itself. Typically people won't hold on for so long with zero physical interaction. It felt hopeless. What was two days going to accomplish for a couple who hadn't even touched in nearly nine years?

We all want to feel safe to be who we are and to feel safe to share our deepest thoughts and dreams. To touch, to love, and be loved is a natural born desire. Somewhere along the way, life happens, and we engage in bad patterns that cultivate disconnection.

Becoming a "love magnet" is discovering how to foster a safe relationship with our partner. A person who's a strong love magnet engages the natural desire of people to connect and be open. And being a love magnet will increase intimacy both emotionally and physically.

The first job for the couple mentioned at the beginning of the chapter was to implement the strategies in this chapter. Once they began behaving and communicating with each other in a "love magnet" manner, things started to turn around, and turn around quickly. By the end of the first day, they were sitting close enough to each other that their legs touched on the couch. During the morning on the second day, they were already holding hands!

The point of any relationship, and especially a marriage, is to be connected and satisfied. No one gets married in order to spend the next five to seven years being utterly miserable. Your first thoughts when meeting your partner were not, "Wow! Now that is someone I could hate in about five years." But something does happen for many couples - irritation, bitterness, and lack of intimacy take over the relationship, and most of them end up divorcing because they despise each other.

If this is you, and your marriage is on the rocks, take hope our friends! The best news of all is that your partner, no matter how emotionally drained, is naturally bent toward wanting to be connected to you. It does not feel like it now, because until now, you did not know how to properly love each other. But once you begin behaving like a love magnet, your partner will be incapable of keeping their heart closed. It will spring back open when it feels safe again.

Why? Because your hearts are designed to be connected. When they are disconnected, your hearts are in an unnatural position.

Your heart resists being closed because it's not comfortable being closed. It wants to be open. This is great news! Your hearts are just waiting to spring open!

How to Pursue Attraction

Pursuing attraction is like being a love magnet is someone who behaves in such a way that people are drawn to them. And, like a magnet, when you learn how to treat your partner in four key ways, you will become irresistible.

As a love magnet, your job is to create safety through these four key ways:

1. Respecting boundaries
2. Valuing your partners' differences
3. Being truthful and honest
4. Being a servant

I (Michael) recently got the opportunity to travel to Ireland and Italy with my wife and two dear friends. What you might not know about us is that we got married at a very young age. I was only 21, and my wife, 22, when we said, "I do." We were so young when we first started off on the adventure of marriage. But to make things even more interesting, we decided (by total accident) to get pregnant on our one-year anniversary. By the tender ages of 23 and 24, we were already parents to boot!

That means, for pretty much the entirety of our married life, we have had children with us.

We were so excited about our trip because all three of our kids were going to be wonderfully occupied for a month. Our oldest, Cole, was in China with one of my best friends, living the life of a missionary. Our two younger children, Reagan and David, were at Kamp Kanakuk for a month. The stars aligned for Amy and I to take the trip of a lifetime for our 40th birthdays!

There was only one major problem; we got into the biggest fight a few months before the trip. You've already learned how imperfect even the experts can be. And let me tell you...we were imperfect. The fight is not the point of this example. It's how we decided to take on the trip and take charge of our time together. *That* is the point of this illustration.

Many couples get into bad arguments before a vacation or major fun-time activity, and we are no different. About three weeks prior to our takeoff, Amy decided to share how nervous she was about our trip because of the issues we'd been dealing with. Because I wanted our trip to be emotionally, spiritually and physically more fun, I was able to put our differences and conflict aside and do the "love magnet" thing to help her feel at ease about the trip.

It all started with Amy being honest about whether or not we would be able to enjoy the trip properly. It was the right thing for her to do. You cannot have a good experience if you keep your feelings or needs hidden from your partner. How I responded, was also good. I started with personal responsibility, like you've already learned, and finished with a dash of "love magnet."

The conversation is still very clear to me. My first thought was, "Well, you..." but I know how destructive a conversation can get when fingers are pointed. Many times our first thoughts are anything but healthy, which is why you want to slow things down and not simply "react" to situations or things your partner says.

My next thought was, "What can I say to help Amy feel more confident about the trip and not worry about whether or not I'm going to ruin it with conflict over our issue?" If you're going to be a love magnet, then you have to learn how to make others' feelings and needs highly valuable. All I said was, "Honey, I know we've been off pretty badly lately, but I want you to know that you are far more valuable to me than any of the junk we've been fighting over. I have no desire to ruin this trip with conflict, and I want you to know that I refuse to ruin this trip by getting into any negative stuff. I'm committed to having fun with you, no matter what." It was a good speech, because she cried good tears. I was a love magnet in that moment because I placed high value on Amy. Things tend to go well when you highly value each other!

The Four Keys to Becoming a Love Magnet

1. Respecting Boundaries

What Amy was asking for was a boundary. The key point in this discussion is that if your partner is wounded because of your actions, then you'd better do a good job at allowing your partner to heal properly, or respect the boundaries they have in place while they heal.

Boundaries can take on different forms.

In our case, the boundary Amy asked for was respecting the fact that she wanted to have fun, and not ruin our vacation because I might not be able to put aside the conflict for a moment and concentrate on loving her as she needed.

Sometimes a boundary is space, sometimes it's tabling a conflict for a short period of time, and sometimes it's a full on wall that has been built by your partner.

Remember this, only the person who built the wall can take it down. By approaching the wall and not building one yourself you set the other person up to naturally pull theirs down. "I understand you are hurt and need some time. I want you to know when you are ready to talk, I will be too."

2. Value Your Differences

When it comes to your personality styles and interests, there are many differences that can be seen as a deficit or asset. The problem many couples have is that they focus on their differences and see them as negative, or as problems. But that is simply not the case. Your differences make you stronger! In an age of compatibility, it can make some couples nervous when they don't feel "compatible."

Compatibility is not the most important thing to relationships. Valuing each other and not trying to change each other's personalities is what makes a marriage worth having. It is a choice to view your partner as a blessing or a curse.

If you want to be a love magnet, now's your chance to start valuing who your partner is, and stop trying to change them.

When we say things like, "Sheesh! Why can't you just relax?" We are sending our partner an unconscious message that says, "I don't like who you are, and I want you to change...in fact, I wish you could be more like me!" It is okay to challenge our partner in areas where something is dysfunctional, and it is impacting us personally. I (Michael) am a major avoider when it comes to conflict. So Amy sharing with me how that makes her feel is a good thing. Amy sharing with me how much she wishes I were more aggressive with people is a bad thing. I'm not an aggressive person, that's Amy's territory. Me telling Amy to "relax" is also not a good thing. I'm trying to tell her she should be more like me, and that does not make a partner feel safe.

Take some time right now to think about who your partner is, and what you appreciate about him or her. Write those things down, make a list, and keep it handy. When you get irritated with your partner, pull out the list and remind yourself how valuable he or she is, and your attitude will take a major turn.

3. Be Truthful And Honest

You send yourself and your partner the best message when you are striving for the best in your life. The cornerstone for living a life worthy of your marriage is honesty. Other words for honesty are integrity, sincerity, and candor. What great words!

Your partner won't know how to be disconnected from you if these are words she can use to describe you!

Jonathan Hilton said this about honesty, "Always Be Honest - How much is your integrity worth? What can you gain by being dishonest that you can truly enjoy? If your word is worth nothing, then neither are you."[14] We would add, "Your relationship is worth nothing as well." The problem with lying to your partner is that you are trying to avoid something or gain something from the lie. But answer me this, is it really worth gaining anything through deceit? All you've gained through lying is more lies and the eventual meltdown when the truth comes out. And trust us...the truth always comes out.

One of my (Michael's) favorite things to say at the beginning of a Smalley Marriage Intensive is a "soap box" speech I have about lying. I love to watch people squirm uncomfortably when I talk about how the truth ALWAYS comes out, no matter how sophisticated or smart the liar is.

On another note, you might remember one of the most successful con men in American history, Bernard Madoff. He is the former non-executive chairman of the NASDAQ stock market, and the admitted operator of a Ponzi scheme that is considered to be the largest financial fraud in U.S. history. But did you know about Charles Ponzi? That's right, Madoff may be the most successful Ponzi scheme in American history,

---

[14] Hilton, Jonathan. "Rules For Life." Mind Connections. 2016. Accessed March 14, 2016. http://www.jonathanhilton.com/life/philosophy/rules-for-life/.

but could you imagine being (or being married to) the man for whom the Ponzi Scheme[15] was named after? Now that is a legacy you do not want to be associated with. These two men became famous for their lies, they might be the best of all time, but both men had something else in common. They both got caught!

You don't want your marriage to be a legacy of lies. Just like Ponzi and Madoff got caught in their deceit, eventually, so will you.

A legacy of lies will eventually make things worse. There is no other possible outcome. A 'no' uttered from the deepest conviction is better than a 'yes' merely uttered to please, or worse, to avoid trouble. You think by not being honest you are saving your partner from hurt, but in reality, you are causing significantly more pain and suffering by being disingenuous. You do not have to go to the catastrophic levels like Madoff and Ponzi to ruin people's lives. A common problem in marriages is partners who believe they are "saving" their partner from undo hurt. If you are being dishonest, then you are only increasing the amount of hurt your partner is going to experience once the truth finally comes out - and it always comes out.

---

[15] Hilton, Jonathan. "Rules For Life." Mind Connections. 2016. Accessed March 14, 2016. http://www.jonathanhilton.com/life/philosophy/rules-for-life/.

You can also be honest in addressing your negative beliefs with each other, especially when they are false negative beliefs (ones that are not even accurate).

4. Be a Servant

If people are not taking personal responsibility in a relationship, then convincing them to be a servant to their partner is like trying to convince people to kill baby seals for new boots and a handbag! (For the record, we love baby seals.) The first reaction we get, many times, when bringing up the idea of serving a partner to a couple is, "Are you kidding! I couldn't serve him because he'd take advantage of me!" Or another classic is, "I've tried doing that, and it didn't work."

Know this, being a servant does work. But many of you have believed serious lies about the consequences of serving. You've convinced yourself that it is not possible in "your marriage" or "your situation." However, it is possible, and it does make a major impact in your relationship.

People are generally concerned about serving others because they fear being taken advantage of. This is not a ridiculous fear, but it is semi-unfounded. Does your partner take advantage of you from time to time? Yes. This does not mean they will FOREVER take advantage of you. It means they made a mistake, they more than likely know this, and their heart is not interested in taking advantage of you. Try and think back to a time someone served you well, authentically put your needs ahead of their own. Maybe it was a grandma, uncle, or cousin. How did you react or respond to this person?

That's right...you probably responded extremely well because you like how it feels when someone serves you; thus desiring to return the favor. This is a general rule of life and relationships. What goes around comes around, whether good or messed up. If you act immaturely, you are setting your partner up to act immaturely. If you do a great job being a servant, you are setting your partner up to be a servant back to you. Nothing is guaranteed, because as you already learned, we cannot control our partner or others.

There is nothing more attractive, hot, sexy, fun, wonderful, or satisfying than a partner who works at being a great servant. You want to be irresistible? It starts (and ends) with being a great servant. Being a great servant is not impossible, and actually, as you begin implementing servanthood in your relationship, you will find it is quite rewarding. A life lived only for yourself is a lonely life. A life lived working at finding opportunities to serve the people around you is more satisfying than you can imagine.

To be a great servant, learn to ask what you can do for your partner in those critical moments where you have caused hurt or your partner is hurting from someone else's actions. Sometimes great hearts and wonderful intentions go very, very badly. You may be getting excited about finally realizing there is a way to act that might just give you the relationship of your dreams. We caution you not to rush forward without making sure you actually know what would be meaningful or significant to your partner. Have you ever tried to do something nice for your partner, to only have it blow up in your face? If you answered yes (which most of us surely do) the problem was not in your heart or intentions, it was in your strategy. **Never assume you know what your partner needs when it comes to serving. Ask.**

If you want to do something loving and serving, you'd better make sure it is what would be meaningful to your partner. This is easily accomplished with a question. You see a need, like your partner just hung up the phone with a parent, and he looks distraught. Don't fly ahead and start doing things you think would be serving. Because in reality, what you think, without asking your partner, is probably only going to be meaningful to you. The next time you want to do something good for your partner, try asking, "Hey...it looks like that phone call was upsetting. Is there anything I can do for you right now?" If you want things to change quickly in your relationship, then start asking that question on a weekly basis and watch what happens.

Go and do it.

Do not be afraid to take the leap, especially if things are stressed out. We promise you this, things are not going to get less stressed by continuing the same behaviors and attitudes that got you in this mess in the first place. Be bold and courageous. Choose to be a servant, even if your partner is not serving you. We have an entire experience in Pursue Intensives on implementing good and healthy boundaries (that is just too long for the book). Don't worry about getting taken advantage of, because you will know how to protect yourself from a partner who does not respond well to your serving.

Remember, becoming a love magnet is about how you treat your partner, especially in times of trouble and conflict. The more you respect boundaries, value your partner's personality, be honest, and ultimately serve your partner, the more your relationship will thrive. A thriving relationship is what you got married for in the first place!

Becoming friends again

Dr. John Gottman in his book, *The Seven Principles for Making Marriage Work*, discusses in Principle One the idea of healthy couples having a love map. A love map is simply knowing your partner intimately. Understanding their likes, dislikes, friends, dreams, etc. In essence, you want to be intimate friends with your partner. You want to know who you partner is and what makes them tick.

So we are going to help you play a game with each other. It is not a difficult game or one you can fail. It is simply a game where you ask each other questions with the goal being to know each other better:[16]

1. What is your favorite memory of dating me?
2. What food reminds you of me?

---

[16] http://www.lifehack.org/articles/communication/list-100-questions-ask-your-partner-date-nights.html

3. When was the last time you thought about me in a positive way?
4. What is your favorite thing that I do for you?
5. What movie reminds you of us?
6. Which of our kids are most like you? (Or if you aren't parents yet - Do you ever picture having kids?)
7. Do you like kissing or hugging more?
8. What's your favorite non-sexual activity that we do together?
9. What is your favorite thing I ever did for a special occasion for you?
10. When do you feel the most protected and taken care of?
11. What was the very first thing you thought about me?
12. What did you learn about marriage from your parents?
13. What did you learn about physical affection from your parents?
14. What is your favorite book?
15. What is your favorite song?
16. What was your first favorite movie as a child?
17. What do you want to do when you retire?
18. What's another career that you think you would love?
19. What's your favorite memory with your mom?
20. What's your favorite memory with your dad?
21. Where have you always wanted to travel?
22. Did you ever consider a totally different career path?
23. What was your favorite class in high school?
24. What was the best party you ever went to?
25. What's the happiest you ever felt?
26. What's a question you've never asked me?
27. What's your favorite personality trait of your own?

28. Did you collect stuff as a child?

29. Which of your parents did you go to when you wanted to talk?

30. What's the most scared you ever felt, as a child?

31. What's the accomplishment you are most proud of?

32. Where do you want to be living in 10 years?

33. Which of your friends would you choose if you had to be on a desert island with just one?

34. Which of your friends is most like you?

35. Which would you like most: a summer house, a year-long vacation, or a boat?

36. What would you do with a million dollars?

37. What would you do with an extra $1,000 to spend only on yourself?

38. Who was your first crush?

39. Who was your first kiss?

40. Who was the first person to have a crush on you?

41. Do you think of yourself as an introvert or an extrovert?

42. If you could go back in time, what age would you be again?

43. If you could see into the future, what would you want to know?

44. What's your greatest talent?

45. What is your most unique trait?

46. What is the best thing about our relationship?

47. Which of my friends do you think is the most fun?

48. Are you an optimist, a pessimist, or a realist?

49. When you wake up in the middle of the night, what do you think about?

50. As a teenager, did you ever rebel against your parents?

51. Who's the closest person to you in your extended family?
52. Did you ever want more or fewer siblings?
53. How did you siblings shape who you are?
54. What was your favorite date night we ever had?
55. Do you ever wish I could read your mind? When?
56. What things about me make you know I'm the one for you?

Knowing your partner intimately helps you become better friends. You get to know each other better and thus get to love each other better in the process!

This entire chapter on being a love magnet is really about increasing your emotional intelligence with each other. Traditional intelligence has always been measured by assessing your IQ or intelligence quotient. Your IQ is a number meant to measure your intelligence. Some of the best IQ's in history are from people like Paul Allen (IQ level 160), Albert Einstein (IQ level around 190), and Marie Curie (IQ level 180).

But a high IQ does not equal someone who is able to love well. In fact, many times a high IQ can make it harder for someone to relate well to other people. In recent years, Psychology has begun measuring people's EQ or emotional quotient. This measures a person's ability to love well, their self-awareness, empathy, or sensitivity toward other people.

Someone with a high EQ knows how to relate well with others and love them in a meaningful way. This is the goal for becoming a love magnet, to increase your EQ. The questions you just went through and the four steps from the beginning of the chapter help you increase your EQ!

Taking it Deeper

Do we have control over people or do we have influence over them? Which do you think is true and why?

_____

_____

_____

_____

_____

What's an important boundary for you in the relationship?
Discuss that with each other.

_____

_____

_____

_____

_____

How have you been judgmental in your relationship? What has
that done to your relationship?

_____

_____

_____

_____

_____

Pursue God Together

My (Michael) father's favorite verse in the bible was Romans 12:10 ESV, "Love one another with brotherly affection. Outdo one another in showing honor."

What does it mean to "outdo one another in showing honor"?

_____

_____

_____

Ask each other how you could "outdo one another" in showing honor? What are specific ways you could show how much you value and honor each other?

For Me   For You

_____   _____

_____   _____

_____   _____

_____   _____

_____   _____

We started off the book with 1 Corinthians 13, which is the overarching theme to *Pursue Oneness*. We want you to read verse 13 again:

> Three things will last forever—faith, hope, and love— and the greatest of these is love.

Why is love the greatest? What have you learned so far in this book to help answer this question?

_____

_____

_____

How do the specific strategies in this book help live out this scripture?

Personal Responsibility

_____

_____

_____

Validation

_____

_____

_____

Timeouts

_____

_____

_____

L.O.V.E. Talk

_____

_____

_____

Becoming a Love Magnet

_____

_____

Activity

We want you to ask each other about different ways you would feel loved. For example, you might finish this statement, "I would feel loved if you..." Write down your partner's answers below.

I would feel loved if you:

_____

I would feel loved if you:

_____

I would feel loved if you:

_____

I would feel loved if you:

_____

Activity

Now you need to do at least one of the items you wrote on the last activity for your partner today. Even if you aren't in the mood to do so, give it a try. Sometimes we have to fake it till we make it. Your choices will dictate your feelings.

Write down what you chose to do for your partner today.

_____

How did it go?

_____

_____

_____

Activity

Ask each other another question, "What would be some ways I could serve you more during the week?" This is a great opportunity to learn specifically what you can do that would be meaningful for your partner. List them below:

I could serve you this week by:

1. _____

2. _____

3. _____

How can you begin to implement some of these ways to serve each other in your relationship?

_____

_____

_____

_____

Activity

Be intentional on serving your partner. You just made a list of things you could do to better serve your partner during the week. Which one do you want to go for today?

_____

_____

_____

_____

Fun Activity

Do something fun today. Check out these conversation starters:

- When do you think I first fell in love with you?
- Who do I consider my closest friends?
- What are the little things that make me happy?
- Where do I dream of going on vacation?
- What is my most favorite movie?
- What am I most proud of?
- What do I identify as my worst habit?
- What do I consider my best body feature?
- What is my biggest fear?
- What do you think 'you do' that turns me on the most?

How did your fun time activity go?

_____

_____

_____

_____

_____

Chapter Journal

What have you discovered after reading and experiencing this chapter?

_____

_____

_____

_____

_____

_____

_____

_____

_____

_____

Key Strategy #7 - Pursue Forgiveness

GOALS FOR THIS CHAPTER

You Will:

- Gain knowledge on the steps of seeking forgiveness
- Understand the process of forgiving your partner
- Learn how to "flush" the bad stuff out

"Resentment is like drinking poison and then hoping it will kill your enemies."
        Nelson Mandela

"If you forgive those who sin against you, your heavenly Father will forgive you. But if you refuse to forgive others, your Father will not forgive your sins." Matthew 6:14-15

Your foundation is firmly set. Your relationship is back in your hands. You understand where conflict comes from, buttons, and the four destructive reactions that lead to divorce. Now let's turn our attention back to the journey of learning both better and different ways to react when buttons get pushed.

Pursue is not a step-by-step journey and neither is marriage.

There are times when specific skills and concepts we are laying out for you in Pursue will be more relevant to your relationship. The success of your marriage is dependent upon your willingness to learn these skills and concepts, but more importantly, we just want you to remember to come back to Pursue when you are feeling stuck. You cannot possibly learn and remember everything. But what you can do is be committed to the importance of being a lifetime learner. If you are willing to stay engaged in the growth and learning process, then your marriage will never remain stuck or miserable for very long.

You will find a way, and Pursue is giving you the absolute best of what we know to repair any conflict your relationship may run into.

The next logical step in the journey of Pursue is to take you down the road of forgiveness. Many people don't understand how forgiveness is a skill. It is something you need to learn, practice, and apply to your relationship. There are times when forgiveness will be minor, an easy process; and times when it will be a major undertaking. But make no mistake, forgiveness is not an emotion, it is knowledge and skill.

Love. . . What a powerful experience to know you are with the one person you believe to be the only person right for you! There's a magical moment when you realize you can't imagine ever spending another day without this person next to you. Every thought is consumed with fantasies and incredible expectations for the future when you first meet and start dating...then you get married! Sound familiar? No one can possibly prepare us for the realities of married life. The joy, the intimacy, the pain, the sorrow; it is all mixed in there to make up the most wonderful relationship on earth.

However, the most wonderful relationship on earth comes at a price. With great intimacy comes great conflict. Great conflict means you need to learn how to properly forgive each other, and as one of our mentors, Dr. Ed Laymance, says, "flush out" the bad stuff that happens between you. Forgiveness is your way to reboot the relationship. But in order to forgive properly each other, you need a proper understanding of forgiveness.

We live in a broken world. We are going to make mistakes that not only affect ourselves, but the people around us. Particularly the people that are most important to us, and there is no relationship more influential than the marital relationship.

Countless times in the life of a marriage, there's a need for forgiveness. From the trivial to the monumental wrongs that happen between two people, forgiveness is the way forward.

Forgiveness is a necessity for any relationship, but especially for a husband and wife.

But why is forgiveness important?

We offer three major reasons why forgiveness is important for your relationship with your partner.

1. You and your partner are incredibly valuable.
2. Forgiveness is the essence of love.
3. Forgiveness is freeing to the soul.

The first reason forgiveness is important is because you and your partner are incredibly valuable. There's an innate value, a deep value bestowed upon us. Because we are valuable, it is important to forgive each other. Forgiveness tells your partner that she or he is worthy to be forgiven. They are important enough for us to forgive. Think back to a time in your own life when a father, mother, brother, sister, or dear friend asked for forgiveness. What kind of memory do you have of that moment? What feelings did experience? It likely felt like a million dollars (or in today's economy, a trillion dollars).

Forgiveness is important because it says you are valuable to me.

Secondly, forgiveness is the essence of love. When we decide to forgive our partner of wrongfully harming us, we are deciding to love him or her unconditionally. The French writer and moralist, François, Duc de La Rochefoucauld, wrote in the 1600's, "We pardon to the extent that we love." If we choose not to forgive, then we are putting up limits and boundaries (conditions) to our love for our partner.

Thirdly, forgiveness is freeing to the soul. Forgiveness allows us to break the bonds of anger, rage, hatred, and vengeance. All these lead down the path of destruction. They are like toxins to the soul, and forgiveness is the cleanser. Much of the work in therapy often focuses around the issue of forgiveness. Anger, rage, hatred, and vengeance prevent us from growing to become the mature adults we desire to be. Without forgiveness, these negative emotions will not only destroy every relationship you have, but they will destroy your physical body. Many studies have been done to show the negative effects, physically, of unresolved anger, including everything from heart disease to liver failure and everything in between.

And although most people understand that forgiveness is a necessary part of a great relationship, people are often resistant to forgiving others.

"Why can't I forgive?" is a question on many people's' mind. "I know I need to, but I just can't find the strength to go through with it."

The short answer is simple. Forgiveness is not an easy task. We believe there are typically three main roadblocks to forgiveness.

Roadblocks To Forgiveness

The first roadblock to forgiveness is a lack of responsibility when it comes to owning up to our dysfunction. If we are unable to see our own faults and mistakes, how can we possibly move toward forgiveness in our relationships? We must first be able to admit that we are not perfect and that we are capable of hurting our partner.

Secondly, unresolved anger is a major hindrance to the healing power of forgiveness. If we refuse to let go of bitterness, rage, or hatred, we are holding on to very destructive forces. These forces are in direct contrast to the power of forgiveness. The two forces cannot exist together. They are too much of a dichotomy for there to be harmony between them.

Finally, many people have great misconceptions about what forgiveness is and therefore struggle with forgiveness because they're on the wrong path. Delusions about forgiveness are dangerous because they are not the truth. The truth will always set us free, like forgiveness. But if we believe the lies about forgiveness, then it is natural that we would avoid it at all costs, especially in the light of real emotional pain.

What are the common erroneous beliefs about forgiveness?

First, and most importantly, forgiving is not forgetting. How many times have we heard someone say, "Forgive and forget!" This is next to impossible, barring serious brain injury, of course. Luckily our brains are not wired to completely forget painful events in our past. Not forgetting allows us to remember saddening and hurtful experiences from our past. Kin Hubbard once wrote, "Nobody ever forgets where he buried a hatchet." Which means we can grow and learn as individuals from the pain we go through in life. Why would we want to forget? That assumes that bad things that happen to us made our lives worse off, but that is simply never true. What doesn't kill us makes us stronger. Right?

If we believe we can stuff away our hurts, we are only prolonging the inevitable. By stuffing our hurts deep down in our inner self, we are simply waiting for the explosion to occur; like a volcano, the intense heat and pressure from past hurts builds up, hoping for release, until it finally erupts. Watch out, these eruptions are extremely damaging to family and friends. The ashes and lava will cover everything in its path.

Six months pregnant, Jenny knew she was in trouble. Nowhere to turn, she lived from shelter to shelter carrying her child and an intense, hidden anger against her father. "You'll never amount to anything!" he used to shout at Jenny when she faltered. "You're worthless!" she heard time and again. But Jenny said she was immune to it. "It doesn't bother me," she would tell her friends who tried to offer what little support she had.

Jenny didn't understand why she continually fell on to bad luck. "Why is this happening to me?" she would say. Seventeen years later, lying half awake on the hospital bed, after several hours of surgery to repair her devastated liver from her alcoholism, Jenny learned. Her daughter, approached her bedside and gently laid her hand upon Jenny's sweaty brow.

"I forgive you," was all her daughter said. "I forgive you." Suddenly Jenny understood why she suffered for so many years. Just three simple words, but a lifetime of pain not wanting to say them. Not wanting to let go of the anger, to let go of the hurt feelings and the shattered ego. This is why we choose to forgive.

William Menninger wrote: "Forgiveness, then, is not forgetting. It is not condoning or absolving. Neither is it pretending nor something done for the sake of the offender. It is not a thing we just do by a brutal act of the will. It does not entail a loss of identity, of specialness, or of face. It does not release the offenders from obligations they may or may not recognize. An understanding of these things will go a long way towards helping people enter into the forgiveness process."

Seeking Forgiveness

Seeking forgiveness from your partner will be a huge part of your marriage. The need to seek forgiveness in a marriage is natural. There will be times of hardship or times you'll be under emotional strain, but as long as the two of you are committed to seeking forgiveness, the hard times become benefits, not deficits.

When seeking forgiveness, you will want to keep three things in mind. First, remember your approach sets the tone of the conversation. Our voice should be soft and receptive to our partner's feelings and attitude. Everything needs to be soft from our tender touch to the sincerity in our voice. We like to ask ourselves, "How humble am I right now? How willing am I to hear what my partner might say?"

An important point to keep in mind: If you have rehearsed a rebuttal, you're probably not ready to forgive or seek forgiveness. Too many times we want to blame others for the hurt WE cause. Blaming only invalidates our partner, and as you learned, lack of responsibility is a major factor in divorce. This is not the time to come with guns blazing and the pulpit roaring.

Secondly, ask specifically how you hurt your partner. Often we can be wrong about how we hurt our partner. This is a major step toward validating our partner's feelings and needs when we ask them how they were hurt by our words or actions. This allows our partner to share their feelings, and if they don't want to share them at the moment, then take time to let them build their thoughts. Or, you can even ask questions that might help your partner more clearly communicate how you hurt him or her.

Thirdly, don't consume your energy worrying about what your partner did to you. We are not in control of our partner, and thus we can't make them seek forgiveness nor accept our own forgiveness. We can only control our own lives and how we behave toward our partner. By humbly seeking forgiveness and acknowledging every aspect of wrong doing on your part, you are cleaning up your end.

And let us clear up something else. Forgiveness is not a one-time event. It is a process, and too many people get this point confused. We often hear, "If he forgave me, then he would be over this by now!" This is just not realistic. If we've done something extremely hurtful, and need to seek forgiveness, then we can't expect for the healing to happen immediately. Your partner will not get over the hurt right away, it takes time. Just because you have earnestly sought forgiveness and forgiveness has been given does not mean that there will not be consequences for your actions.

In fact, depending on the severity of the hurt, the person we hurt may never fully recover from the pain. This is not to say we (or they) will always be suffering, but it does mean the pain might show up periodically, even years later, because of some event that sparks a memory. The pain isn't as severe as when it first happened, but it still hurts.

I (Michael) can remember a man who approached me at one of our monthly marriage enrichment seminars. He was holding the hand of his wife, and they looked normal enough to me. His eyes were somewhat reddened by the tears he'd shed at this point in the seminar. His wife looked somewhat impartial to the whole experience.

I said hello and the husband started right in. "I don't think I've forgiven my wife yet because I'm still hurt and angry over what she did to me." He said this while grasping her hand in a tender and loving way to assure her that he loved her. I was impressed by their obvious commitment to each other.

Something in their eyes made me feel they were in it for the long haul in their marriage. So I asked him what had happened that he needed to forgive of his wife, and she just remained silent as he described an incredible story.

She confessed to having multiple affairs during their 20-year marriage, which was obviously extremely hurtful and damaging to her husband. She promised him that they only occurred in the first few years of their marriage and that she'd never had another affair. I was surprised that the wife could hold out for so long in keeping this secret of an affair from her husband for over 15 years, but then the hammer dropped, and I knew exactly why she'd kept it a secret.

Near the end of his explanation, he quickly said something that utterly shocked me, "And she's not sure if our 15-year-old daughter is mine." Wow! I couldn't believe it. This man was faced with the possibility that his daughter of 15 years may not be his biological daughter! I couldn't believe that he was still holding his wife's hand in love. I'd be doing something very different if Amy revealed something like that to me.

I asked him when he found out about the affairs and the possibility that his daughter may not actually be his, and what he said astounded me, especially in light of his initial question about how he did not feel like he'd truly forgiven his wife yet. "Two weeks ago." He said calmly and straight-faced.

Two weeks! I couldn't believe he was bothered by the fact that he'd not completely forgiven his wife yet. What surprised me the most was that he wanted to know why he still hurt so much after forgiving her. This is the problem many people face in regards to forgiveness. They somehow get the belief that once those magic words, "I forgive you," are spoken, that all pain and hurt will just disappear. But this is not the case. We must go through an entire process before we can actually begin to heal from the hurt caused by our partner or anyone for that matter.

The process of forgiveness is just that, a process. And there are two sides to that process as well. There is the person seeking forgiveness and the person who must do the forgiving. We have already talked about being the person seeking forgiveness. Now let's tackle the subject of being the person being asked to forgive.

The Process of Forgiving

We like to use Menninger's model of forgiveness[17] because we feel like it is the most complete and Christ-like process of forgiveness. And although offenders can seek forgiveness, they are not ultimately in control of whether or not the victim forgives. Forgiveness is entirely in the hands of the victim.

If you choose to follow these next five steps in the process of forgiveness, understanding that you may move in and out of each level throughout the process, we know you will greatly increase your ability to forgive. And learning to forgive *is* an

[17] Menninger, William. *The Process of Forgiveness*. New York: Continuum, 1996.

ability. It's not a feeling, an emotion, nor something that happens by chance. It is a learned skill and best achieved with practice.

Stage One – Claiming the Hurt

The first step in the process of forgiveness, as outlined by Menninger, is claiming the hurt. This might seem obvious, but for many people, living in denial and or forgetfulness is much easier than admitting something has happened to us that is painful. We often try to avoid the painful experiences in our lives, because they are painful. In psychology, it's called the pleasure principle. All humans behave in a manner to maximize pleasure and minimize pain. We don't want to experience pain, so we avoid it by ignoring it, disguising it, hiding it, stuffing it, and a whole host of other defense mechanisms all designed to protect us from pain.

Sometimes avoiding the pain is a direct consequence of our laziness. We don't want to devote the energy necessary to deal with the issue, so we avoid it. M. Scott Peck has said that laziness is the biggest sin and the path toward human pathology. I (Michael) believe him to be true because I know that when I sin or avoid things, I don't want to do the work of a healthy person. It goes back to the clean slate idea. My wife loves a clean house, and I have to admit when things are clean I can finds things better. But cleaning takes time, and just like cleaning your physical house takes time so does cleaning your emotional living space. To be healthy takes a lot of good decisions. Our nature is to sin, so we are constantly desiring to do things that are not good, and we must expend a lot of energy to fight those things off. The apostle Paul asked, "Why do I do the things I hate, and not the things I know are good?" As they say in today's world, the struggle is real.

The first step, again, is claiming the hurt. See what the pain has done in your life. It's about opening our eyes to our lives, and not living in denial. This is important because we've admitted that something needs to be done. How can we forgive someone if we don't acknowledge that something needs to be forgiven?

Stage Two - Experiencing Guilt

Now that you've claimed the hurt and are taking full responsibility for how you feel and how the hurt has affected your life, the next stage in this process of forgiveness is typically experiencing guilt. It is common to feel responsible for what happened. "What could I have done to prevent what happened," or, "If only I hadn't. . ." Both thoughts are very normal and necessary in the process of forgiveness.

By recognizing your hurt feelings, you give yourself the opportunity to have power over it. You now know what it is that is causing your emotional pain. Something to help you during this stage of the process is to do something for yourself that makes you feel valuable. Often times, victims of hurt feel worthless and powerless, and doing something specifically for yourself will help bring you out of the stage of guilt. It's about getting active and not remaining passive during this process.

You have to "do" something, move in a direction, in order for change to occur.

Couples wonder why nothing is getting better in therapy sometimes because they are still doing the same things that got them into trouble. We have to change our behaviors in order to experience change.

Stage Three - The Victim

You've claimed the hurt and experienced the possible guilt, you are now ready to feel like a victim. Yes, we know that sounds crazy, but it is the next step toward forgiveness and your ultimate healing. Now that you've recognized your hurt, it is only natural to feel victimized. Signs of this stage are depression, listlessness, isolation, or bitterness.

When we experience these kinds of emotions it is only natural to want to medicate them. It's the human way to solve our emotional pain. We get involved with drugs, alcohol, food, and anything that makes us feel momentarily better. But the key is that it is only momentary, it is never lasting.

This stage is a cry for help. It's a 911 to your soul. The best thing to do during this stage is to seek support from others (support group) and do things for other people. Helping others helps you get outside yourself and focus on others, which ultimately helps you feel more in control and less like a victim.

Stage Four – Anger

People want to ignore feelings of anger because at some time during our lives we got the impression that anger was bad. Anger is not bad! In fact, it is extremely healthy, when handled in a healthy way. Anger motivates us to change and take action. It's like the fuel in the process of forgiveness. It gives us energy to make it through the process of forgiveness. What is inappropriate anger, you might be asking?

When anger is focused on vengeance, then more than likely it is not a healthy anger. Anger shouldn't be about getting back at somebody, but rather about getting motivated to change. Vengeance will destroy us. It's like toxic waste to the soul. Its very nature is hateful, and hate only encourages more hate.

The key to processing anger is being healthy in your anger. You never want to simply "let yourself go" in your anger, which allows it to take root in your soul and blocks your relationship with others. Positive anger lets us know something needs to be taken care of. It's like the red warning lights in your car. When the lights are blinking, you'd better take notice of the problem. Pent up anger might not cause problems right away, but let us assure you, it will grow and sprout up someday to hurt and damage the people around you.

Stage Five – Wholeness

Now is the time you can actually forgive as an act of love because you haven't denied yourself the opportunity to grow through all the stages of forgiveness. You're no longer a victim of your pain because you've taken control over it. Forgiveness is the ultimate sign of maturity and love. Forgiveness says that you know you're not perfect, and neither is your partner. So you choose to love them anyway, and you forgive them so you are free to grow in your life and in your relationship together.

Wholeness is a direct product of the first four stages. It's not even a choice; it's a product of the first four stages of forgiveness. You don't grab on to wholeness. It grabs you. You cannot help but become whole when you go through the first four stages! That is the power of the journey of forgiveness, in looking at forgiveness as a process instead of a one-time event. When you forgive each other, you give the marriage a chance at experiencing what you want the most...joy, peace, harmony, sexual intimacy, fun, etc. It is the act of forgiving which allows you to be heroes to each other. Heroes in love.

Taking it Deeper

What happens to us if we choose not to forgive?

_____

_____

_____

_____

_____

What are three major reasons forgiveness is important?

_____

_____

_____

_____

_____

What, things, if any, do you need to forgive in your life? People, circumstances, kids, etc. Write it down below.

_____

_____

_____

_____

_____

Is there anything you need to seek forgiveness about? Write it down below.

_____

_____

_____

_____

_____

Pursue God Together

Why does Jesus make such a big deal about forgiving others, especially as it relates to our own relationship with Him?

> And whenever you stand praying, forgive, if you have anything against anyone, so that your Father also who is in heaven may forgive you your trespasses. Mark 11:25 ESV

Jesus said in Matthew 6:15 ESV, "But if you do not forgive others their trespasses, neither will your Father forgive your trespasses."

To understand this verse, John Piper wrote:

> It means: No one who cherishes a grudge against someone dare approach God in search of mercy. God treats us in accordance with the belief of our heart: if we believe it is good and beautiful to harbor resentments and tabulate wrongs done against us, then God will recognize that our plea for forgiveness is sheer hypocrisy—for we will be asking him to do what we believe to be bad. It is a dreadful thing to try to make

God your patsy by asking him to act in a way that you, as your action shows, esteem very lowly.

How might Piper's quote challenge what you thought when reading Matthew 6:15

_____

_____

_____

Read the following verses:

> But to you who are willing to listen, I say, love your enemies! Do good to those who hate you. Bless those who curse you. Pray for those who hurt you. Luke 6:27-28

Write down a prayer of forgiveness for your partner, to help get you started we are including one from Kristine Brown (www.crosswalk.com):

> Dear Merciful Lord,
> Thank you for your gift of forgiveness. Your only Son loved me enough to come to earth and experience the worst pain imaginable so I could be forgiven. Your mercy flows to me in spite of my faults and failures. Your Word says to "clothe yourselves with love, which binds us all together in perfect harmony." (Col. 3:14)

Help me demonstrate unconditional love today, even to those who hurt me.

I understand that even though I feel scarred, my emotions don't have to control my actions. Father, may Your sweet words saturate my mind and direct my thoughts. Help me release the hurt and begin to love as Jesus loves. I want to see my offender through my Savior's eyes. If I can be forgiven, so can he. I understand there are no levels to your love. We are all your children, and your desire is that none of us should perish.

You teach us to "let the peace that comes from Christ rule in our hearts." (Col. 3:15) When I forgive in words, allow your Holy Spirit to fill my heart with peace. I pray this peace that only comes from Jesus will rule in my heart, keeping out doubt and questions. And above all, I am thankful. Not just today, not just this week, but always. Thank you for the reminder, "Always be thankful." (Col. 3:15) With gratitude I can draw closer to you and let go of unforgiveness. With gratitude I can see the person who caused my pain as a child of the Most High God. Loved and accepted. Help me find the compassion that comes with true forgiveness.

And when I see the person who hurt me, bring this prayer back to my remembrance, so I can take any ungodly thoughts captive and make them obedient to Christ. (2 Cor. 10:5) And may the confidence of Christ in my heart guide me into the freedom of forgiveness. I praise you for the work you are doing in my life, teaching and perfecting my faith. In Jesus' Name, Amen.

Your own prayer of forgiveness:

_____

_____

_____

_____

_____

_____

_____

_____

_____

_____

_____

Activity

Dr. Ed Laymance's "Flushing" Exercise

We've mentioned Dr. Laymance several times in this book. We are thrilled to provide his "Flushing" exercise as a part of the chapter on Forgiveness. Never has there been a better personal exercise to help you truly forgive than "Flushing." The title says it all! Dr. Laymance helps you flush out the hurt from past relationships and move forward in a dynamic way through the process of forgiveness.

He gave us permission to include his special exercise on forgiveness. Our hope is if you are still feeling stuck from painful experiences and relationships in the past, you will give this exercise your complete and undivided attention.

Find a place where you can be alone for at least an hour. Then simply start at the beginning and be faithful to each of Dr. Laymance's steps. If you get stuck or the hurt becomes too much to bear, please consider working with a pastor or professional counselor. You could also contact us toll free at 800-975-8748 to schedule a private intensive with one of our coaches across the United States.

Dr. Laymance's own ministry is Impact Counseling located in Arlington, Texas. You can visit his website at www.impactcounseling.com. A little more about them from the website:

*We are a faith-based counseling and guidance center
that welcomes all - regardless of religious background
or experience. Our mission is to help you find your way
from difficulties and dissatisfactions to the peace,
purpose, joy, and fulfillment God desires for you.*

The Flushing Exercise

When someone hurts or harms you in some way, it is much like
having something thrown at you that belongs in a toilet. You've
got three choices with what to do with it. (1) Pick it up and
throw it back - have a fight with it - get it all over yourself -
wear it and wonder why life stinks. (2) Pick it up and smear it
all over yourself - wallow in it - wear it and wonder why life
stinks. (3) Put it where it goes and flush. Don't wear it and
don't stink!

If you don't know how to flush or simply choose not to, in time
you've got quite a problem. Life becomes like a house flooded
with six inches of raw sewage. Spend all the money you want
re-decorating and paint the walls any color you like, but it
won't matter. You can't get past the smell!

Unless you get rid of the raw sewage that life has thrown your
way (release resentments, heal hurts, and dump
disappointments), it won't matter where you go, what you do,
who you're with, what you have - the stink never goes away.
Before you "redecorate" life (change how you think, feel,
choose, etc.), get rid of the sewage.

So let's begin with people who do and do not forgive.

Why You Do Not Forgive

- You don't know how.
- You don't feel like it and don't want to.
- The person who hurt you does not deserve it or has not earned it.
- You don't believe anything will really change.
- If you forgive, you can no longer justify your actions.
- You will have no ammunition for the next conflict.
- Playing the "blame game" requires change for others but not for you.
- You believe that forgiveness is an emotion to feel.
- You believe that you are keeping the one who hurt you in "emotional jail" - punishing them until justice is served.

Why You Choose To Forgive

- You learn how.
- You don't wait until you feel like it.
- You realize the person who hurt you will never truly deserve it or earn it because you will always remember.
- You don't settle for the way things are. As someone once said, "No one can go back and make a brand new start, my friend, but anyone can start from here and make a brand new end!"
- You stop justifying your actions. You no longer allow the actions of others to determine how you live.

- You declare a "ceasefire" for the next conflict, regardless of what others do.
- You learn that with the "blame game," the only winning move is not to play that game.
- You understand that forgiveness is a decision you make, not an emotion you feel.
- You realize that the one who hurt you is not in "emotional jail" – you are! They have gone on, and you're holding yourself hostage – where is the justice in that?

Releasing resentments, healing hurts, and dumping disappointments is for you, not those who sinned against you. You are not letting them go free, you are letting yourself go free! They may never admit their sin, ask for forgiveness, seek to make things right, or change. It doesn't matter because this isn't for them anyway!

The best illustration of this principle I have heard is a true story. A woman was abducted, raped, robbed, shot and left for dead. When the abductor shot her he put a gun to her head intending instant death. She jerked at the last moment. The bullet went sideways. He ran off and was never found. She survived the attack and endured months of surgeries and rehab. She was interviewed by a reporter about three to four years after the attack. In the middle of the interview, the reporter commented how she must really hate the man that put her through all this. Her response was, "I once did, but not any more." When the reporter asked for an explanation she replied, "For a long time, I was consumed with revenge and justice. I wanted him caught. I wanted him to endure all the pain and suffering he had inflicted upon me. I could think of nothing else. Then one day it occurred to me that man had robbed me of one night in my life. I decided I was not going to give him one more day!"

Wow! That's it! When you continue to wear what someone else has thrown your way, you're letting them reach from the past into your present and control your future. It's time to get past the past. It's time for life to smell better. It's time to flush! Some of the strongholds the enemy has in place are connected to resentments, hurts, and disappointments. Let's get rid of them by having what I call "**emotional funerals**."

1. Ask yourself, "Is there anyone, living or dead, that I feel owes me something? Am I holding a grudge or bitterness against someone? Do I carry disappointment with me? Is there anyone, living or dead, who hurt me or harmed me, and I'm wearing that hurt?"

2. On a pad of paper, make a list of the names God brings to mind. Don't be surprised if your name is on the list. You may be carrying guilt or shame for something you allowed. Don't be surprised if God's name is on the list. You may be confused, angry, or hurt that God allowed bad things to happen to you or someone you love. After five to ten minutes, you will have a list.

3. Tear off that page and set it aside. Start with any name on your list and put that name at the top of a clean sheet of paper. Then ask God to show you what it is about this person that you

need to release."

4. Write down everything that comes to mind. This is not a novel, so you need not start at the beginning of the relationship and work forward. One thought will connect to another. Write what comes. Use words, phrases, paragraphs, and symbols – however you want to do this. This is for no one's eyes but yours, so be brutally honest. Hold nothing back.

5. Some of what you write will be connected to other people on your list. Just make a note by their name; you will add this to their list later. Keep on task with one person at a time.

6. This is pretty emotional stuff, so you will need to take an occasional break. Take a walk, blow your nose, hit a pillow, and get a drink - but stay with it until you feel like you are done.

7. What you're going to do next may seem silly or stupid. Do it anyway. This is a very important step. Make sure you are alone and no one can hear you. Imagine the person you've been writing about is sitting in a chair close by. You need to stand, so you can walk around. I want you to see yourself as a judge. What you have written is a list of indictments against that person.

As judge, read out loud everything you've written; with whatever emotions you feel; using whatever words and volume you need to use. This is a "no holds barred," "up close and personal," "in their face," "full force" kind of experience!

Don't be "Christian" or "appropriate." Let 'em have it! Include any additional things that come to mind. Say exactly what you feel.

8. Some of what you've written only needs to be said once. Some of what you've written needs to be said more than once. Say what you've written until it no longer needs to be said - a hundred times if necessary. One of the reasons you've been carrying this stuff is because it needed to be said, and you needed to hear yourself say it - without debate, rebuttal, excuse, or explanations from the one who hurt you.

9. When you get to the last word on the last page, having expressed all the emotions you needed to express, as judge, declare out loud, "Guilty as charged!"

10. Then, as judge, declare out loud, "Case dismissed!"

11. Next, pray, "God, I do not feel like dismissing this (because you don't!), but I don't want to be controlled by this any longer. I choose to forgive and release it to you. I choose to "flush." Now, help me walk away from how I feel and enjoy the sweet smell of freedom! Amen."

12. Destroy what you've written as a physical representation to yourself that the case has been dismissed. Dig a hole and bury it, burn it, shred it, whatever feels good. One person I helped said when they were finished with everyone on their list, in addition to destroying what they had written, they wrote each name on an individual sheet of toilet paper and flushed

each one. What a great idea!

13. Repeat this process until you have had an "emotional funeral" for everyone on your list. Don't stop until you have flushed everything. One inch of raw sewage is better than six inches, but the house still stinks!

Questions Concerning Forgiveness

Question 1
Once I've forgiven the ones who hurt me, do I need to confront them?

No. This is for you, not them. If a relationship also needs to be reconciled, confrontation may be necessary later, but not now. Focus on living free from the pain of your past. Reconciliation is best accomplished when you are emotionally free.

Question 2.
Do I go and ask forgiveness?

No. We have been talking about how you were hurt by someone else. If you have hurt someone, that is another matter.

Question 3.
I can forgive, but I can't forget. Is that OK?

Yes. In fact, you should not forget. If you forget, then everyday is like the movie Groundhog Day. You are doomed to keep repeating the same thing over and over. You want to remember.

Remembering is insulation to protect you and keep you from "going there" again.

Question 4.

If I do not forget, then how can I get past the hurtful memories?

Our senses "trigger" emotions that are connected to memories. All you need do is see, hear, taste, touch, or smell something that reminds you of a hurt and immediately you "feel" the hurt again.

For example, a young lady was seeking to get past a sexual assault. Her progress took a step back when she attended a reunion and hugged an old friend. Memories of her assault shot through her with the hug. He was not the abuser – but he did wear the same cologne the abuser wore. The smell of the cologne triggered the hurtful memories.

Each day you may encounter triggers, many of which are subconscious. After you have released resentments, you must determine to defuse them.

Question 5.

Okay, then how do I defuse the triggers?

You can defuse triggers only after you have had your emotional funerals.

After your funerals:

- Pre-decide on two or three things you would want to spend time thinking about, rather than the hurtful memories - a trip you're looking forward to taking, something you enjoy doing, etc.
- When something triggers a hurtful memory that you have already released, tell yourself the truth. Yes, that happened. Yes, that hurt.

Yes, guilty as charged, but case dismissed. God has that now, not me, and I'd rather think about one of the things I've pre-decided on instead. This is called the principle of replacement. You are not trying to ignore what happened or play like it never occurred. It did happen. But because you have chosen to release to God how you felt, now you can choose to think about something you would like to think about rather than the hurtful memories.

Each time you do this, you will cut in half the power of that particular trigger and diminish its ability to control you. If you pay attention to the triggers and purpose to take away their power, gradually you will put distance between you and the hurtful memories until you remember the occurrence but are no longer controlled by the pain.

It will be as if the hurtful memories are King Kong standing over you - with bad breath! The good news is you can get in your car and drive away. King Kong's feet are in concrete, and he can't chase you. The bad news is your car's going about two miles an hour. However, as you continue to drive away, King Kong's size reduces in the rearview mirror. He never disappears over the horizon (you never forget), but he is no longer huge and foreboding.

If you daily practice the principle of replacement (after the emotional funerals), you will experience God's freedom from the control of hurtful memories.

Question 6.
This helps me with the past, but how do I get rid of new hurts? How do I "flush" daily?

When hit with a hurt, the initial response is to react. This is true of physical pain (like stumping your toe), and this is true of emotional pain (like experiencing rejection). Although reacting to pain is a natural response, actions, not reactions, are necessary to heal the hurt. You need a way to get the emotions "out of your face" (reaction), so you can see what happened and determine what you can do to change how you feel (action). Here's a way to move from reactions to actions.

1. The natural emotions you feel are the result of a want, need, or expectation not being fulfilled by people, places, and things in your life. For example, you wanted your friends to understand how you felt, but they did not. You needed a nice quiet evening at home, but it did not happen. You expected the new car to be better than the old one, but it was worse.

2. How you feel about what happened needs to be expressed. Feelings are best expressed when you combine four ingredients - physical, verbal, private, and appropriate.

Let me give you a bad example of what I mean. You do something that makes me very angry. I grab a glass vase and smash it on the floor in front of you while telling you how I feel. That was physical - I threw something; it was verbal - I said how I felt; but it was not private - I did it in front of you; and what I did was not appropriate - I just broke something! However, I could go for a ten-minute walk (physical); by myself (private); say under my breath what I'd really like to say to you (verbal); and that's an OK thing to do (appropriate).

There are many appropriate physical activities you can do while expressing your emotions in private: housework, yard work, exercise, driving (as long as your foot is not heavy on the accelerator!), etc. Like the emotional funerals, what happened needs to be said. You may be able to flush how you feel in ten minutes. It may take ten hours, or even ten days, but say it aloud until it does not need saying anymore.

Once the initial emotions are "out of your face," you can focus on, rather than react to, what happened - the wants, needs, and expectations not being fulfilled.

Determine what you can do to change how you feel. Sometimes all you are able to do is choose not to be controlled by the actions of others.

Decide what is needed to change things. Do you need information, patience, an explanation, confrontation, etc.?

Then take action. Attack the problem, not the person.

Activity

You already wrote down things you might need to seek forgiveness over. Now we encourage you to approach that person or those people and seek forgiveness.

This is not easy, but it is so necessary if you want to experience life to the fullest. Write down again whom you are going to approach.

_____

_____

_____

_____

Journal your experience on the next page as to what happened when you approached someone for forgiveness. How were you received by them? Did you learn something about yourself?

If someone doesn't receive your approach for forgiveness, be patient and allow them time to heal. It might be too fresh for them, or they have allowed the hurt to turn into bitterness. Either way, you can always go back after a little bit and try again.

Seeking Forgiveness Journal

How were you received by them? Did you learn something about yourself?

_____

_____

_____

_____

_____

_____

_____

_____

_____

_____

_____

Activity

What if you've gone through the process of forgiveness but still get caught up in the hurt of the specific wound? Maybe you have triggers that remind you of the hurt; specific places, certain people, whatever it is, there might be things that remind you of the pain.

Do not be discouraged. This activity is meant to keep you on track. Write down any triggers you might have that remind you of the wound below.

_____

_____

_____

_____

Now, with each trigger, tell yourself once again what the truth is! **The truth is that you have forgiven**. You can tell yourself, "Yes that hurt, but I have dismissed it. It has been released." Instead of dwelling on the negative of the hurt, tell yourself what you want to feel. We don't talk to ourselves enough. There's a lot of power in speaking to yourself in the positive.

Fun Activity

Do something fun today. In case you need some help getting the conversation started, here you go:

- If you had intro music, what song would it be? Why?
- What three words best describe you?
- What would be your perfect weekend getaway?
- What's your favorite number and why?
- What's the favorite thing you own?
- What in life brings you the most joy?
- Where's the most beautiful place you've been?
- What's your favorite season and why?

How did your fun time activity go?

_____

_____

_____

_____

_____

Chapter Journal

What have you discovered after reading and experiencing this
chapter?

_____

_____

_____

_____

_____

_____

_____

_____

_____

Pursue Intimacy

GOALS FOR THIS CHAPTER

- Discover the importance of date nights
- Understand the benefit of date nights

"Those who cannot change their minds cannot change anything."
George Bernard Shaw

"A glad heart makes a happy face; a broken heart crushes the spirit." Proverbs 15:13

Date nights. Couples know on a surface level they are important, yet few couples consistently do date nights. Date nights are not a high priority. Kids, work, errands, kids again… okay, one more time, and KIDS make date nights less than a priority for most couples.

This has to change. Date nights matter in the overall health and level of satisfaction for couples. Date nights should be as important as parenting and kids' schedules. If you are not having fun together, you are not having fun! When you are not having fun, your relationship struggles. When your relationship struggles, divorce becomes an option. You don't want to be miserable, therefore, if you are never having any fun together and consistently getting into conflict and not resolving issues, divorce is just-around-the-corner.

If you are wondering why we are making date nights such a priority, then you might not be aware of Dr. John Gottman's work[18] on happy couples. He found, after researching many couples who reported being happy after at least 20 years of marriage, that those couples have a 5:1 positive to negative ratio. This means that couples who are married for the long haul, and who are happy, have five good things happen to every one negative thing.

Conclusion...you really need to be able to have fun together. No excuses. We don't care if you're stressed out with each other or can't find babysitting - we will not take no for an answer.

If you don't believe us, then believe a major study on the importance of date nights done by W. Bradford Wilcox & Jeffrey Dew. Their study was analyzing the research on date nights in their article, "The Date Night Opportunity: What Does Couple Time Tell Us About The Potential Value Of Date Nights?"[19] They gave five ways date nights help couples and marriage:

---

[18] Gottman, John Mordechai., and Nan Silver. *The Seven Principles for Making Marriage Work*. New York: Three Rivers Press, 1999.

[19] Wilcox, Bradford, and Jeffrey Dew. "The Date Night Opportunity - National Marriage Project." Accessed March 15, 2016. http://nationalmarriageproject.org/wp-content/uploads/2012/05/NMP-DateNight.pdf.

1 Communication

One of the crucial ingredients to a successful relationship is an open channel of communication. Date nights give couples an opportunity to talk with each other free from distractions. Date nights allow a couple to foster shared dreams and develop goals for their relationship in to the future.

Date nights can help partners to "stay current" with each other's lives and offer one another support for meeting these challenges. Date nights should foster much-needed communication, mutual understanding, and a sense of communion between partners.

2 Novelty

Most couples experience a decline in relationship quality after a few years, partly because they become habituated to one another and are more likely to take one another, and their relationship, for granted.

A growing body of research suggests that couples who engage in novel activities that are fun, active, or otherwise arousing—from hiking to dancing to travel to card games—enjoy higher levels of relationship quality.

3 Eros

Most contemporary relationships begin with an element of eros —that romantic love that is linked to passion, excitement, and an overwhelming sense of attraction to one's beloved. But with time, the emotional and physical manifestations of erotic love tend to decline in most couples. (Helen Fisher, Why We Love: The Nature and Chemistry of Romantic Love (New York: Henry Holt, 2004).)

Date nights can strengthen or rekindle that romantic spark that can be helpful in sustaining the fires of love over the long haul. All of these things can foster higher levels of sexual satisfaction in their marriage or relationship.

4 Commitment

Husbands and wives, as well as other romantic partners, are more likely to enjoy stable, high-quality relationships when they experience a strong sense of commitment to one another and to their relationship.

Date nights can solidify an expectation of commitment among couples by fostering a sense of togetherness, by allowing partners to signal to one another—as well as friends and family —that they take their relationship seriously, and by furnishing them with opportunities to spend time with one another, to communicate, and to enjoy fun activities together.

5 De-stress

Stress is one of the biggest threats to a strong marriage or relationship. Stress related to work, finances, parenthood, or illness can prove corrosive to a relationship, insofar as it causes one or both partners to become irritable, withdrawn, violent, or otherwise difficult to live with.[20]

Date nights can be helpful for relieving stress on couples, as they allow them to enjoy time with one another apart from the pressing concerns of their ordinary life. Clearly, husbands and wives who enjoy high levels of couple time together are markedly less likely to divorce.

Their conclusion, "Our analyses indicate that couple time is indeed associated with higher reports of satisfaction with communication, sexual satisfaction, and commitment for both husbands and wives. Couple time is particularly beneficial to couples with children at home, insofar as it is more of a precious commodity for these couples."

If you truly want things better in your relationship, you will make time each week to have fun with each other. This is why we had you take time for fun activities after each chapter!

What would keep you from going out?

Unresolved conflict and bitterness will always be at the heart of resistance to having fun with your partner. This is why we saved the chapter on date nights for the end. If you are not doing the work to love each other well, you will not want to go out with each other.

---

[20] Rand Conger et al., "Linking Economic Hardship to Marital Quality and Instability," Journal of Marriage and Family 52 (1990): 643–656.

An important note here is that you don't have to "want" to go out with each other in order to have a good time. Does this statement feel shocking to you? It shouldn't, because it directly relates to what we taught in the chapter on personal responsibility.

Date nights with each other are an important part of a healthy relationship…especially when your relationship is hurting or in conflict. You can take a timeout (which you learned) and choose to go out and have fun together. The question is whether you are willing to put aside your differences for an evening and focus on fun.

The last thing you want to do for your relationship is to resist having fun together. A date night is an opportunity for the two of you to turn things around and get some positive momentum going for your relationship. Just focus on the following things that will help you keep it fun and positive on a date night:

- Keep the time conflict free. We will often turn to each other before a date night or fun activity and high five each other. It may sound corny, but it establishes for both of us that we are going to do everything we can to keep conflict out of the fun time together.
- If something negative happens, call a timeout and tell each other that you will resolve it later after the fun time. Remember that you can put those negative feelings aside and focus on having fun, especially when you know you can L.O.V.E. Talk it later.

You can also go on a date with fun conversation starters if you struggle communicating with each other. Tracey Eyster wrote an article for Family Life where she shared "30 Ways To Start A Conversation With Your Spouse." These are a great way to begin a good conversation[21]:

1. My funniest memory of our dating days is when …
2. Our kids would freak out if they knew we …
3. Before we are together in heaven, I pray that here on earth we …
4. I have this memory of you in a certain outfit. Remember …
5. The most scared you have ever been was …
6. The happiest you have ever been was …
7. I remember thinking I was courageous when I was young because I …
8. I used to always wish I could …
9. If I could spend a day just talking to any one person, it would be …
10. I wish I had learned to …
11. I picture us old, sitting in a rocking chair and you looking over at me and saying, "Daggum it, we never …"
12. If I could spend 24 hours doing anything in the world with you, it would be …
13. I like it best when you refer to me as …
14. The song that always makes me think of you is …
15. My sweetest memory of us in our youth is when we …

---

[21] http://www.familylife.com/articles/topics/marriage/staying-married/communication/30-ways-to-start-a-conversation-with-your-spouse

16. My favorite memory of our wedding day is …
17. My greatest need right now as a woman is to …
18. My greatest need right now as a man is to …
19. If I could have any super power, it would be …
20. If I could eat anything and it not affect my health, I would feast on …
21. If I could have lived during a different time period, it would be …
22. I laugh every time I think of you doing …
23. I would so enjoy reading out loud together …
24. If we could be roadies for any musical talent, I would choose …
25. If I had it to do over, I would propose to you by …
26. The world's best anniversary trip would be to go to …
27. My favorite photo of us is the one where …
28. Did you know that it scares me so much to …
29. When we fell in love, my favorite thing about you back then was …
30. I feel you love me the most when you …

Armed with these conversation starters, you can experience a fun and healthy date night!

But maybe conversation starters aren't enough to help motivate you to go out on a date with each other. Focus on the Family has some great ideas for date nights we want to share with you! These aren't all of them, but you can find the rest of their ideas here:

http://www.focusonthefamily.ca/marriage/great-date-ideas

A few of our favorite date night ideas from Focus on the
Family:

Classy classifieds

Give each other $5 to spend, or to just pretend to spend. Look
through online classifieds, such as Craigslist.org, and see who
can find the best deal, worst rip-off, or oddest buy!

Break a record

Bond with your spouse by breaking a Guinness World Record
– or at least trying! It's easy to get started. Just visit
Guinnessworldrecords.com and search for records that you
think you have a shot at. Maybe you can eat the most grapes in
one minute? Or spin a coin for the longest time?

Real estate date

Whether you're on the house hunt, or comfortably settled in
your home, perusing real estate listings with your spouse is
free, fun and a great way to spark conversation! From home or
a coffee shop, search online real estate websites such as
Realtor.com. Browse a variety of price ranges and property
sizes, and brainstorm your plans and preferences for the
architecture, interior design and landscaping of your dream
home!

Surprise date adventures

Keep your spouse guessing by turning date night into a surprise
adventure. To begin, make a set of cards (either decorated and
written by hand or done on the computer) with one activity
listed on each. For example, one could list a movie, and the

others could list a restaurant, a dessert café, or a stop by his or her favorite store to pick out a small treat. Each card would then be sealed in an envelope. Present the envelopes to your date and have them choose one out of your hand. Whatever they pick, do it! Repeat the process until all the date options have been chosen.

At-home spa

Give your love some tender care by planning a relaxing massage date. To create your at-home spa, set up a quiet room with candles, flowers, and light, classical music. Fill the room with a light scent, preferably an essential oil burning in a diffuser. Then, have your spouse lie on the bed with fresh sheets, and begin with a head and neck rub, followed by a back massage. Be sure to take your time and ask your spouse what pressure they prefer and what spots need the most attention. If you want help with your massage skills, there are plenty of books available to give you tips. But don't worry! Whether you know how to give a perfect massage, giving a gift of loving touch is a surefire way to convey love and care to your mate.

The more the merrier

A double date with a twist! Have the husbands become one date-planning team and the wives become another. With your date-planning partner, collaborate your ideas for a super-secret creative date for your spouses. Who knows what new and exciting ideas you'll come up with when you brainstorm date ideas with a friend?

Taking it Deeper

Why is taking time to have fun together important?

_____

_____

_____

What are some of the most fun times you've had together?

_____

_____

_____

What would fun-time look like for the two of you today, in light of your current life stage?

_____

_____

_____

Who are other couples you would enjoy hanging out with, and why?

Couple:_____

Why

_____

_____

Couple:_____

Why

_____

_____

Couple:_____

Why

_____

_____

Pursue God Together

Read the following verses and then write down how you are going to respond to the verses specifically. In other words, what are you going to do to live out the verse with your spouse?

Ecclesiastes 5:18-20 MSG, "After looking at the way things are on this earth, here's what I've decided is the best way to live: Take care of yourself, have a good time, and make the most of whatever job you have for as long as God gives you life. And that's about it. That's the human lot. Yes, we should make the most of what God gives, both the bounty and the capacity to enjoy it, accepting what's given and delighting in the work. It's God's gift! God deals out joy in the present, the now. It's useless to brood over how long we might live."

I will…

_____

_____

Proverbs 15:13, "A glad heart makes a happy face; a broken heart crushes the spirit."

I will…

_____

_____

Wrapping Up

GOALS FOR THIS CHAPTER

- Remember what you learned
- Apply it to your relationship

"What you get by achieving your goals is not as important as what you become by achieving your goals."
> Zig Ziglar

"Above all, clothe yourselves with love, which binds us all together in perfect harmony." Colossians 3:14

The goal for all of our books is to inspire transformation in your most important relationships. To help you build a better relationship through practical tools.

Where do you go from here?

You learned from the beginning of this book that the knowledge and skills contained in these pages were all developed and perfected through the Smalley Marriage Intensive for hurting couples. This means the content has been battle-tested and proven to work! You can be confident when using any of the tools or skills in this book, because we know they work.

The next step for your relationship is up to you. Are you willing to put into practice the knowledge and skills you learned in this book?

Change can be a daunting quest. It's scary because you don't know what the future holds. You might be asking yourself, "Will our relationship really change for the better?" The good news is that change is up to you! Change is not up to your partner because you are only in control of you (see skill #1 The Foundation).

We ask couples frequently in the Smalley Marriage Intensive a powerful question, "What do you think will happen if you change and start loving your partner well?" The answers back are always the same! They respond by telling us they think their partner will probably respond back in a loving way. And they are correct!

When you love someone well, they naturally want to love you back. It does not mean this happens 100% of the time, but it certainly sets you up to be loved well. What other choice do you really have, anyway? Loving well is the only choice we have in relationships. Regardless of how we are being treated.

Jesus said in Matthew 7:12 (ESV), "So whatever you wish that others would do to you, do also to them, for this is the Law and the Prophets."

The roadmap to your relationship's success is in how well you love each other. This book has given you proven knowledge and skills to love each other like you both deserve.

We want to close the book by asking you to do one more thing. On the next page is the Lifetime Commitment Contract. We want both of you to sign it. There's nothing more powerful than two people unwaveringly committed to each other!

Developing A Lifetime Commitment Contract

The goal when creating this contract is to establish several mutually agreed upon steps to undertake before seeking a divorce. For example, you can agree on the minimum number of marital counseling sessions, decide which friends could serve as a support and prayer group, and possibly list which marriage books or videos need to be read. You can make a commitment not to be romantically involved with anyone during this period, include the specific number of months to wait before a divorce, agree whether to get a legal separation first, voiding the contract for physical abuse, and so forth. The key is to brainstorm every possible step to take before seeking a divorce. You might even have several other couples who would be willing to make the same commitment to brainstorm with you.

The final point is to determine the consequences if the contract is not honored. Usually, financial ramifications work the best. We encourage you to get your pastor, friend, or lawyer's signature on the finished document.

You may be thinking, "Divorce…that will never happen to us!" We know how you feel. We've made a commitment that divorce will never be an option. However, feelings change.

There will be times that you will not feel "in love" with your partner. For whatever reason, you may even consider separation or divorce. We need to do everything within our power to guard against making decisions based on fluctuating emotions. Having a written contract can help you make the right choices to strengthen your relationship and to keep your promise of "til death do us part."

(next page for example lifetime commitment contract)

EXAMPLE LIFETIME COMMITMENT CONTRACT

Necessary Steps To Staying Healthy:

Step One
We agree to get involved in a small group through a church for at least six months.

Step Two
We agree to read at least two marriage-related books (like any of the ones suggested at the end of *Pursue Your Marriage in Two Days*).

Step Three
We agree to ask the following people to begin praying for us and for our marriage:

_____   _____

_____   _____

Step Four
We agree to attend a Smalley Marriage Intensive or marriage counseling first, before ever considering divorce.

X _____   X _____
  Husband   Wife

LIFETIME COMMITMENT CONTRACT

Necessary Steps To Staying Healthy:

X _____ X _____
  Husband   Wife

_____
Date

Michael & Amy Smalley

Michael and Amy specialize in teaching couples the principles of loving well and loving for a lifetime. Their popularity as nationally renowned relationship experts quickly grew through their straightforward, no-nonsense advice, and humor.

Their love story began while they were undergraduates at Baylor University in Waco, Texas. Michael's love for Amy was immediate, but Amy, however, took some more convincing. So Michael went to the ends of the earth (by becoming a college male cheerleader because Amy was on the Baylor Yell-Leading squad) to finally win her over. After graduation, they went on to earn master's degrees in clinical psychology from Wheaton College in Chicago, Illinois. Michael finished his Ph.D. at Barnham Theological Seminary.

They currently serve as co-founders of the Smalley Institute. Their popular Pursue Intensive for Couples is currently in eight locations across the United States. The centers help couples reignite their marriage in just two days.

The Smalley's have enjoyed 24 years of marriage and have three children Cole, Reagan, and David.

Roger Gibson

Roger and his bride, Kari recently celebrated twenty-eight years of marriage. He's proud to be called dad to Michael, Hannah, and Zoie in Keller, Texas where he is the Marriage and Family Pastor at Fellowship of the Parks.

Roger has the privilege of helping couples prepare for marriage, strengthen existing marriages and restore broken relationships.

He worked for 20 years as the Vice President of Gary Smalley's ministry, served as Senior Director of Adult and Family Ministries for the General Council of the Assemblies of God, and is the founder of Man Up and Go, a father to the fatherless ministry.

He is a known fanatic for Jesus, family, college basketball, and tacos.